2 0 1 0 3 *W* 5 0 4

PART OF WALES

ardif

BRISTOL CHANNEL

Flatholmes
pholmes

Portshead P.

St Thomas's H

SOME...
Div...
HUN...
Containing the Cities, Buroughs and
Market Towns, with the Roads & Distances
By Eman. Bowen
Geograph.r to His Majesty

PART OF
GLOCESTERS.

BRISTOL
Cainham
Broadwells
Wrington
Donn
19
18
D
Axbridge
A
C
E
G
Avon R
BATH
I

Pensford

Mendip
Chewton Mendip
Wells Hills
Cheddar
Cliff Okey Hole
M

F
C
20

Phillips Norton
15

H

30

20

Culver
Sand

dgwater Bay
Stert P.

somer

R

Huntspill
Breat Marsh
Brent
D
10
K
R
R

5
Sedgmore
Glastonbury
The Tor
Brent
R

Shepton Mallet
Maiden Bradley

O
Y
X
Frome

Selwood
Forest
M
Wi
Bruton
a

10

ck Hills
g

Tone
S
Parret R
Pold
U Down
Moor Lands

Somerton
22
c
d
N. Curry
Langport
Ivel R

Castle Cary
Wincaunton

Z PART

Taunton
7
f
e
l
Ilchester
o
p

b
h
N

OF

on

Ilminster
S Petherton
m
Crookhorn
n
q

r
Yeovil
Milbourn P. ort
to London

own Hills
Chard

Ax R
to Weymouth
to Seton

DORSET SHIRE

British Statute Miles
3 6 9 12

5'

50

IRE

2 0 1 0 3. *West Longi* 5 0 *-tude from* 4 0 *London* 3 0

e of Arts and Sciences, for W. Owen at Temple Bar.

# Minehead and Dunster

# MINEHEAD and DUNSTER

## Lois Lamplugh

## Phillimore

1987

Published by
PHILLIMORE & CO. LTD.
Shopwyke Hall, Chichester, Sussex, England

ISBN 0 85033 630 9

Printed and bound in Great Britain by
BIDDLES LTD.
Guildford, Surrey

# Contents

# List of Illustrations

## Acknowledgements

Once again, as in the case of my earlier books, *Barnstaple: Town on the Taw* and *A History of Ilfracombe*, I have made repeated use of the library of the North Devon Athenaeum, Barnstaple, and have been grateful for the helpfulness of Mr. J. M. Rowe, Head Librarian, and his staff. I would also like to express thanks to Mr. David Bromwich, M.A., Librarian of the Local History Library, Taunton, and the staff of the West Country Studies Library, Exeter, for answering queries, and to Mr. Gareth Purcell, Editor of the *West Somerset Free Press*, for allowing me to consult files of that newspaper and of the *Minehead and West Somerset Visitors' List*.

I am particularly grateful to Mr. Walter Harris for his kindness in taking the photograph used on the jacket, and for allowing me to reproduce other photographs which appear as nos. 17, 27, 63, 64 and 65. For permission to reproduce other illustrations I would like to thank the following: Mrs. Joan Astell for no. 61 from the Alfred Vowles Collection, and the directors of the North Devon Athenaeum for nos. 50 and 52 and line drawings nos. 25, 33, 44 and 46.

## Sources for Line Illustrations

| | |
|---|---|
| Burrow | Burrow, E. J., *Ancient Earthworks and Camps of Somerset*, London, 1924. |
| Green | Green, Emmanuel, *The Preparations of Somerset against the Spanish Armada*. |
| Hancock | Hancock, Preb., *Minehead*, privately printed, 1903 (drawings by E. Spranklin). |
| Harper | Harper, C. G., *The Somerset Coast*, Chapman and Hall, 1909. |
| Jeboult | Jeboult, E., *A History of West Somerset*, Taunton, 1893). |
| Jusserand | Jusserand, J. J., *English Wayfaring Life in the Middle Ages*, T. Fisher Unwin, 1890. |
| Larter | Larter, C. E., *Minehead, Porlock and Dunster*, Homeland Association Ltd., 1902. |
| Lyte | Lyte, Sir Henry Maxwell, *Dunster and its Lords*, privately printed, 1882. |
| Rock | Rock, W. F., *England Under Victoria*, privately printed. |
| Savage | Savage, Rev. James, *A History of Carhampton*, Bristol and London, 1830. |
| Traill and Mann | Traill, H. S., and Mann, J. S. (eds.), *Social England*, Cassell, 1902. |

*Chapter One*

# Settlers and Invaders

Once, the future site of Minehead lay inland. Until about six or seven thousand years ago, a great forest of oak, yew and ash stretched out over much of what is now the Bristol Channel. Deer, wild horses and cattle grazed there; along both coasts of the Channel their remains have been found among the submerged stumps of ancient trees. Stone Age men hunted them; flints and scrapers of common Neolithic types were found early this century, under the blue marine silt off Minehead and Porlock, in the old surface soil. Little heaps of splinters beside a yew tree stump enabled one archaeologist to write that he could 'mark the exact places where their makers sat'.[1]

Bronze Age men came to the high sandstone ridge, an outlier of Exmoor, that runs for some five miles from the heights of Bossington Hill, above the lovely Vale of Porlock, to North Hill above Minehead. They left a scattering of tumuli or round burial barrows near Selworthy Beacon, the highest point of the ridge. People of the Iron Age left two earthworks: one, Bury Castle, lies on the hillside almost due south of the Beacon;[2] the other is a strange and compelling place above the sea at

1. Bat's Castle, Dunster Deer Park. This Iron Age Camp is roughly circular, with two banks and ditches, and two entrances, one on the west and the other on the east. The view over the Bristol Channel on a clear day is superb. In this drawing, the Conygar Tower can just be seen in the middle distance, and on the left, beyond the dark bulk of Grabbist Hill, appears the outline of North Hill above Minehead (E. J. Burrow).

Furzebury Brake, two miles west of Minehead. Its earth walls enclose only about half an acre; Grexy Combe plunges almost sheer on its eastern flank, with a little stream that may have been the settlement's water supply flowing down it.

The present-day farms of East and West Myne lie only a short distance from this earthwork; they are said to be very old in origin. It has been suggested that Celts farmed here. East Myne certainly appears in the Domesday survey; the relevant entry gives the name of its Saxon owner as Leofwin or Lewin, and records that his Norman successor kept a sizeable flock of sheep and goats.

Dunster, too, had its Iron Age camps, on high ground in what was to become Dunster Park; on Gallox Hill are a one-acre enclosure and a three-acre fort, once ascribed to the Romans and known as Caesar's Camp but now called Bat's Castle. To Dunster came Celtic chieftains and a Celtic holy man, or so a medieval Life of St Carantoc would suggest. The Life, fabricated in a Welsh monastery some six hundred years after the saint's death, speaks of his landing from Wales at Dindreathou, or Dindrarthou, which some writers have identified with Dunster, and finding a chieftain called Cadwy and the young King Arthur ruling there. A serpent, 'most fierce and terrible', had laid waste the surrounding land of Carrum (Carhampton), and Arthur seized the opportunity of begging Carantoc to remove it.

The saint prayed, and the serpent at once came to him 'with a great noise, like a calf running to its mother, and bent its head to the saint with humble heart and downcast eyes'. Carantoc put his stole round its neck and led it into Cadwy's citadel before dismissing it with instructions to harm no one. Carantoc later built a church at the mouth of the little river Willet (now the Donniford stream); this was still in existence in 1180, when it was given to Wells Cathedral.[3]

Cadwy's fortress, if it existed, may have been on the conical hillock of Dunster; it has been supposed that, in later centuries, Saxon chieftains fortified that hill. The name of Dunster's last Saxon lord is given in Domesday as Aluric or Aelfric, and the place appears simply as Torre; the 'dun' element, deriving from a word for ridge or mountain, appears a little later.

Clearly the hillock offered a ready-made motte of unusual size on which the powerful Norman lord, William de Mohun (or Moyon, or Moion), chose to build his castle.[4] He was appointed Sheriff of Somerset, and given no fewer than 68 manors, most of them in Somerset. A large group of them lay in the area around Dunster, including East Myne, Bratton, Alcombe – and Minehead. From the time of the Conquest, the people of Minehead thus found themselves subservient to the lords of Dunster.

There seems to have been no mention of a place-name approximating to Minehead until the 11th century, whereas Watchet, only five miles eastwards along the coast, is known to have been well established in Saxon times; included in the Burghal Hidage of 919, it possessed a mint later in the 10th century, and on several occasions attracted the unwelcome attentions of Danish raiders. Writers from the 18th to the 20th century tried over-ingeniously to derive the name Minehead from that of its Norman lords; J. L. W. Page, in 1890, is typical in insisting that the name was simply a corruption or contraction of Mohun 'with the old Saxon *heved* added'. It has since been pointed out, however, that *Myneheafdon* (Myne Head) appears in a Saxon document of 1046.[5]

William de Mohun sublet many of his manors, but Minehead, like Dunster, he held himself. In 1086 it had 12 slaves, 27 villagers and 22 smallholders. On 12 acres of meadow, 24 acres of woodland and a large area of pasture – about six miles by four – it was reported that there were 16 cattle, 10 pigs, 300 sheep and a cob. So few animals, on such a large acreage, sounds somewhat improbable, as so often in Domesday (only 10 pigs, for instance, on 24 acres of woodland that was probably oak?). There was a mill, worth three shillings a year. There is no mention of fishing or seafaring; 11th-century Minehead appears as an agricultural village.

The descendants of William de Mohun I held their lands for some three hundred years. The most notorious became as ferocious a brigand-baron as any in the disastrous reign of Stephen.[6] He supported Stephen's opponent, Matilda, the chosen successor of her father, Henry I; she created him Earl of Dorset. He called himself Earl of Somerset. The *Gesta Stephani* referred to him as a man of high lineage who had nevertheless gathered together in his stronghold, Dunster, a band of knights with whom he roamed over that part of England 'in hostile manner sweeping it as with a whirlwind'. No man of wealth was safe from him; he imprisoned and tortured them and seized their possessions, changing 'a realm of peace and quiet, of joy and merriment, into a scene of strife, rebellion, weeping and lamentation'.

Stephen hurried west to tackle this turbulent baron, but was apparently taken aback when he saw Dunster, 'inaccessible on one side where it was washed by the sea, and very strongly fortified on the other by towers and walls, by a ditch and outworks'.

Prudently he withdrew, and sent orders to Henry de Tracy, lord of Barnstaple, 'a man skilled in war and tested by many battles', to deal with the rebel. Henry obeyed. Whether he waited until the tide was out or, as has been suggested, the water washing the castle was a temporary flood, he reached and subdued the place, humbled Mohun and captured 104 of his knights.

The late 12th century saw several short-lived generations of the Mohun family. At the beginning of the 13th, Reginald de Mohun died before he was 30, leaving as his heir a 10-year-old boy also called Reginald. In the usual feudal fashion, he became a royal ward. King John put him in the care, first of the son of the Earl of Cornwall and then of his grandfather, William de Briwere, and meanwhile was careful to maintain a garrison of archers and horsemen in Dunster Castle.

When Reginald de Mohun II attained his majority, he seems to have been more attentive to his borough of Dunster than his predecessors. He obtained from Henry III the right to hold a weekly market; this, and the annual fair, took place in North Street, now the High Street. Reginald released buyers and sellers in the market from all tolls or transactions under the value of a shilling, a useful concession at the time, and freed merchants and fishermen from all toll whatsoever.

He seems to have been a pious man. Like his ancestors since the Conquest, he was generous to the Church; among other benefactions, he founded a Cistercian Abbey at Newenham and decreed that a priest should celebrate daily 'to the end of time' in a chapel in the upper part of Dunster Castle dedicated to St Stephen. A puritanical streak is suggested by the fact that he forbade the brewing of strong beer and abandoned his predecessors' claim to a large free allowance of weak beer.

Briefly, on two occasions, he was appointed Justice of the Forests south of the Trent. In 1253 he was granted a charter by Henry II to hunt the hare, the fox, the cat and the badger in all Somerset. Shortly before his death in 1257 he took four stags and three roebucks (capriolos) by writ of the king. It has been suggested that the so-called roebucks were in fact red deer calves to add to the stock in Dunster Park.[7]

His grandson John succeeded him, as his son, another John, had died in Gascony. During the boy's minority the warden appointed to protect Dunster Castle, Adam de Gurdon, fought off invaders who landed at Minehead intending to ravage the county of Somerset. William de Berkeley, 'a knight of noble birth but infamous character', led a large force of Welshmen across the Bristol Channel, but the Dunster garrison beat them off and chased them to the sea; many, including Berkeley himself, were drowned as they struggled to re-embark.

The pattern of short-lived father handing on to very young son continued during the early 14th century. The last male Mohun, yet another John, was born in 1320 and, like his ancestor Reginald, became a ward of the king at the age of ten. He was first put in the care of the Bishop of Lincoln but, presumably thinking it more suitable for a boy of his lineage to be brought up in a knightly household, the bishop handed him on to his brother, Sir Bartholomew de Burghersh. Sir Bartholomew had a daughter, Joan. It is possible that she and John were attracted to one another; more probably, as happened elsewhere in similar situations, a marriage was arranged; at any rate, as soon as he came of age, John de Mohun took Joan de Burghersh as his wife.

He became an experienced soldier, serving in his monarch's wars abroad, originally under the leadership of his guardian, later with John of Gaunt and with the Black Prince. The latter showed him favour by giving him a horse charmingly called Grisel Gris. Eminent among fighting men of his time, a survivor of Crecy, he was created one of the 25 original knights of Edward III's chivalric Order of the Garter.

It was during his lifetime that the borough of Dunster bestirred itself, for the first and only time, to send representatives to parliament, but like some other small west-country towns – for instance, Ilfracombe – the burgesses found it an expense which they had no wish to repeat. John de Mohun himself, as a baron, was summoned to the Upper House.

He incurred debts in London, as his brief will indicates; he conveyed his estates to trustees for the benefit of Lady Joan. Within a year of his death in 1376, Joan was selling the right of succession to Lady Elizabeth Luttrell, a daughter of Hugh Courtenay, Earl of Devon and, through her mother, a great-granddaughter of Edward I. A copy of the document recording the sale of Dunster Castle and the manors of Minehead, Kilton and Carhampton is on display in the castle today; it acknowledges the receipt of 5,000 marks of good money in full payment, and is dated 20 November 1377. Thus, on the only occasion between the Conquest and the mid-20th century that Dunster Castle was sold, it passed from the hands of one woman to those of another.

Lady Joan retained the life interest in the properties. She had no son, but her three daughters all married well. The eldest became the wife of the Earl of Salisbury and the second was three times married, her third husband being Edward Plantagenet, Duke of York. In her widowhood, Lady Joan evidently had no taste for life in her

remote Somerset castle; she chose to spend much of
her time in London and Canterbury. She seems to have
been a remarkable character; it is noteworthy that both
she and her daughter the Countess of Salisbury were
in the habit of appearing at Court arrayed in the robes
of that knightly Order in which her husband had been
enrolled, the Garter.

As Joan outlived Lady Elizabeth Luttrell by nine
years, it was Lady Elizabeth's son, Sir Hugh, who in
1404 inherited the estates to which his mother had
bought the reversion. Described as a man of great
worth, honourably employed by three kings of
England, he held a variety of appointments, including
Steward of the Household to Henry IV's second wife,
Joan, member of the Privy Council and ambassador to
the Duke of Burgundy. He saw much service in France;
in 1401, when he was about 37, he was appointed
Lieutenant of Calais.

On learning that Lady Joan de Mohun was dead, he
lost no time in claiming his inheritance. He spent
Christmas 1405 at his castle of Dunster; a number of
his tenants came to amuse him by performing some
kind of Mummers' play, and he rewarded them with 40
pence; children from his manor of Minehead danced
for him and were given 20 pence.

Lady Joan's two surviving daughters and their
influential husbands, as well as Lord Strange, widower
of the youngest daughter, had no intention of letting
the Mohun lands go easily. They challenged Sir
Hugh's right to inherit. The question dragged on
through more than one hearing, and a trial at Ilchester
in 1406, but somehow, no one knows exactly how, Sir
Hugh finally triumphed – and so Dunster and
Minehead, with all the other Mohun estates, passed
into the keeping of a family which, with one 25-year
break, would hold them for another six centuries.

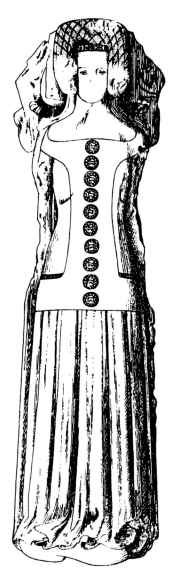

2. Joan de Mohun, 'Lady of
Dunster', died 1404 (Lyte).

*Chapter Two*

# The People of a Medieval Manor: 1. The Working of the Land

Because the Luttrells carefully preserved documents relating to their estates, from their own time and earlier, it is possible to trace the development of Minehead from the age of the Plantagenets. In the late 13th century it still appears as an agricultural holding, worth in all just over £27 a year. The total area is evidently well over 200 acres, mostly arable but with some meadowland as well as pasture for oxen – the usual draught animals – and sheep. The value of the water mill has gone up from the three shillings of Domesday to 20 shillings![1]

A far more detailed document survives from 1300.[2] It shows that the lord's farm was divided into half a dozen areas of varying sizes. The biggest was a field of over seventy acres, worth fourpence an acre, lying south of 'la Lane', the main thoroughfare of the manor leading up from the sea. It stretched as far as the bridge then known as Fullbrygge, crossing the rivulet running down from Bratton. North of the Lane lay an arable field of 42 acres, and there was a slightly smaller field called Wetehulle or Wetenhille. There were two 'parks'; one, of some thirty acres, was probably arable, as it was worth only fourpence an acre, while the other, of 20 acres, was worth three shillings an acre and was therefore almost certainly meadow. Other pastures lay on 'la Fenne', the low-lying marshy ground east of Minehead. In addition there was a small field of nearly six acres 'against the gate of the Court'. This Court may have been the bailiff's house; a 15th-century document speaks of a 'capital messuage' there, near which, after the feast of St Michael (29 September), all tenants were allowed to pasture their beasts until early February. They had similar rights on what was called North Marsh.

Sea weirs, or permanent fish traps, sometimes called pools, are first mentioned in these accounts of 1300. They were constructed of stakes set into underwater walls of stone and interwoven with wattles. The tenants who held them were allowed by the lord to take timber from North Hill at the discretion of his Woodward.

It now begins to be possible to identify individual tenants by name. Some ninety men and 12 women (six of the latter noted as widows) are listed, with the size of his or her holding and its rent. On average, the annual rental of a small holding was about twopence halfpenny an acre, though a few were worth more. The rent of a cottage might be from sixpence to one and sixpence a year. To these rents would be added the value of the tenant's services and in some cases the payment he had to make in kind; at certain times of the year eggs, fowls, wax or honey might have to be provided for the lord's larder, or 'larder money' paid instead. Although no specific mention is made of the mill, it is noted that 'all the men of West Myne [the ancient farm on North Hill, already mentioned] give to the lord yearly twelve pence so that they may grind their corn where they will'. It was evidently worth paying this fee to

6

3. Dunster's one remaining mill, as it was some sixty years ago. The present building, on a much older site, has been restored more than once, most recently in 1979. In working order, and open to the public, it is under the care of Mr. A. S. Capps, a tenant of the National Trust.

avoid the trouble of carrying their corn three miles to be ground at the lord's mill, as every peasant on a feudal estate was then bound to do, paying for the privilege.

Tenants had customary duties to perform for their lord, receiving food and a small payment in return. There was, for instance, Roger Londe, who held one ferling, which on this estate amounted to 12 acres.[3] He had to plough once in winter; the work was valued at twopence halfpenny, but the lord gave him only one penny for it. Roger also had to reap for one day; for this he received three-farthings' worth of bread and *campanagium*, which might be meat or fish or some other food to go with the bread.

The duties of certain tenants were given in detail so that they could be used as exemplars, to save the trouble of writing them all out in respect of other tenants. There is, for instance, a certain Roger de Tracy. The list of his duties is long and varied. According to season, he was to plough, harrow, help to fence 'the land called Barlychland' in front of the gate of the Court, weed the lord's corn and reap it. He had to dig in the vineyard. (The fact that vines were grown at both Minehead and Dunster suggests a pleasantly warm climate in West Somerset in the Middle Ages.)[4] He had to bring his cart to carry hay, corn and brushwood at Christmas, taking some of the hay and a faggot of wood in recompense. Once a year he had to drive his cart as far as Lyme (Regis) to fetch salt, that essential commodity for preserving meat and fish, and twice a year he went to Taunton or Bridgwater or Watchet for seed. He had to cleanse the mill pond 'from the rising of the sun until the third hour', though at what season is not stated. He also had to work for half a day 'to lead the water in the water leat'. Finally he had to make charcoal in the park at Minehead. For most of

4. A reaper's cart going uphill, from the Luttrell Psalter (Jusserand).

5. An English carriage of the 14th century, from the Luttrell Psalter (Jusserand).

these duties he received some payment, or food, or both. Half a dozen other men, all, like Roger de Tracy, holding 24 acres and owning carts, performed the same or very similar duties.

Altogether this document from the time of the Mohuns gives a wonderfully exact impression of peasant life in medieval England. Pictorial representations of that life appear in many illuminated manuscripts, but in none perhaps more vividly than in one commissioned by Sir Geoffrey Luttrell of Irnham in Lincolnshire, an ancestor of the Luttrells of Dunster Castle. (Irnham Street in Minehead recalls the family's connection with the place.) The Luttrell Psalter was completed in about 1340.[5] Although all the little pictures of 14th-century life it contains were probably painted by a monk working in a scriptorium in eastern England, the clothes and customs he saw around him, especially on the land, may not have been very different from those to be found in the west.

The psalter shows all levels of society, from royalty travelling in one of the huge cumbrous covered-wagon-like carriages of the time (drawn with a charming innocence of perspective) to peasants ploughing, harrowing, weeding corn, scaring crows and milking ewes in a crowded pen of wattle hurdles. One drives a cart with three horses in line ahead, but those on the Minehead estate may well have been pulled by oxen, except perhaps on the occasional long-distance journey, like those of Roger de Tracy.

The population of Minehead seems to have been more or less stable in the early 14th century. In 1330 there were just over a hundred tenants, six of them free men, paying a total rent of about twenty-five shillings.[6]

Throughout Britain, over the next 70 years, there were six outbreaks of the plague: the great epidemic of 1348, when an estimated third to one-half of the population died, and recurrences in each decade from 1360 to the 1390s. In Dunster Deanery, covering Dunster and Minehead, there were 26 appointments to benefices between November 1348 and December 1349, where ordinarily there might have been some half-dozen, at most. In the whole diocese of Bath and Wells, in the same period, '201 benefices out of a total number of 413 ... had been vacated and 249 clergy appointed, sometimes for the second, third or even fourth time'.[7] However, as in very many small places, specific documentary references to loss of life on the Luttrell estates are absent.

The first Statute of Labourers, passed in 1351, observed that 'a great part of the people, and especially of workmen and servants, late died of the pestilence'. The survivors, finding their labour in great demand, 'do withdraw themselves unless they have livery and wages to double and treble what they were wont to take, to the great damage of the great men'. The Statute tried to impose a wage freeze, and largely failed. For 30 years there were struggles

6. Ploughing, redrawn from the Luttrell Psalter (Traill and Mann).

7. Sir Geoffrey Luttrell arming for the tournament, redrawn from the Luttrell Psalter (Lyte).

8. Sir Geoffrey Luttrell at table, redrawn from the Luttrell Psalter (Lyte).

between the labouring people and the land-owners, until finally resentment broke out in the short-lived Peasants' Revolt of 1381. The following year saw the plague outbreak of the 1380s.

With these events in mind, it is interesting to see what may

9. Sowing, redrawn from the Luttrell Psalter (Traill and Mann).

be deduced from the accounts of Richard Elys, Bailiff of Minehead, for the year ending at Michaelmas 1384.[8] There are certainly indications of a drop in population. Instead of over one hundred tenants, there are only 70 – and, significantly, many have holdings on the demesne; the lord of Dunster Castle (in fact at this time the lady, Joan de Mohun) can no longer find, or afford, the labour to farm it herself. There are still the big fields north and south of 'la Lane', as well as the field called Wetenhulle and pasture on 'la Fenne', but they have been sliced up into little plots, or more probably typical medieval strips, of one, two or three acres, with a minority of tenants holding as much as four to six acres. Moreover these are not short-term leases, but are held for life.

On the rest of the manor, it is clear that new tenants are taking over: '5 shillings for the farm of Wm. Premere for one messuage and 12 acres of land which Wm. Brod formerly held', '10 shillings for the farm of John Tutthorne for one messuage and 24 acres of land which Rob. Schire held', and so on. In one or two cases this simply seems to mean a swapping about of holdings. Richard Elys the bailiff, for example – who is himself new to his office, replacing a Walter Culle – takes a 24-acre farm formerly held by Roger Childe, while Childe takes a 24-acre farm formerly held by Roger Comesheade. There are other similar exchanges, but at least 15 of the little farms – still divided into fractions of a virgate, 6, 12 or 24 acres – have new tenants, presumably because their former owners have recently died. The bailiff reports considerable arrears of rent, which is also significant. Outside the demesne, the total acreage being worked is only a little over half what it was at the beginning of the century. By contrast, the number of fish weirs or sea traps has increased to ten, and the mill – held by a new miller – has increased in value to 60 shillings a year. The park is no longer cultivated but 'depastured by the wild beasts and cattle of the lady'.

Four women, possibly widows of plague victims, have tiny holdings; Margery Ketle has one acre, Margery Kurslade two acres in the field called Fullbrygge, Sabine atte Forde four acres in the big field south of the Lane and Margery Yeamste two acres in the same field, although she also shares 23 acres in 'la Fenne' with a certain Matt Jacob.

One tenant appears as something of a mystery. Richard Elys's accounts show three entries concerning 'Adam, vicar of the church of Minehead'. No surname is given, either there, or in Chadwyck-Healey's *History of West Somerset*, where it is said that Adam, the vicar, entered the name of a son born to Peter of Bratton 'on the page of the missal' – in Minehead church, presumably – in about 1378. Yet the list of incumbents to be seen today in the church shows that a Mattheus Eliot was vicar from 1348 to 1401 (one cleric who was immune to plague), and that he was followed by Richard Bruton. However Eliot also held the living of Fiddington near Bridgwater. Possibly Adam acted as locum for him; perhaps he was one of the many contemporary secular priests.

Certainly he farmed 24 acres formerly held by Roger Atteyarde, two acres on the demesne south of the Lane, and land at Wetenhulle with a meadow at Full-brygge. He paid only 6s. 8d. for the 24 acres

10. Harrowing, redrawn from the Luttrell Psalter (Traill and Mann).

and the house on it, but as much as 32 shillings for the other land; on the demesne, rents were some four shillings an acre, compared with a few pence on the manor in general.

A good deal of work service had been commuted to money payments, following a national trend. The bailiff accounts for money received for certain works of ploughing, harrowing, carrying corn and hay, reaping and tending the vineyard. At the same time he notes down a considerable number of works still carried out. Some rents were still partly paid in kind; at least two tenants held 'by script of the lord for rent of one rose and five shillings'.

Within a generation numbers were increasing again. A rent roll of 1407, soon after Sir Hugh Luttrell had won possession, shows 116 names, and there are 31 more in the hamlets of Periton, Woodcombe, Hindon, Lynch, North Ridge and East and West Myne, all within the manor. By 1428, the year Sir Hugh died, there were said to be 120 messuages each worth 12 pence a year, as well as 'six messuages called Botehouse, each one whereof is worth per annum clear fourpence', and seven of the permanent fish traps along the shore.

The annual fair at the feast of St Michael, 29 September, is reported to be worth only 20 pence per annum; this sounds like a slip for 20 shillings as, in 1383, when plague had reduced numbers, the tolls and profits of the fair had brought in 14 shillings. By this time the park extends to 150 acres, arable land to 200 and meadow to 40; there are in addition 400 acres of furze, heath and waste, worth a penny an acre. All of this suggests a considerable change in land use in the previous 40 years, with the moorland increasing and being used simply as pasture.

Works are still being carried out by some customary tenants; they include '182 manual works called Churrys', worth a farthing each. This word *churry*, sometimes written *churr*, meaning a turn or piece of work, was the forerunner of the modern English char. It has lingered as the name of a thoroughfare in Minehead. In 1654 Churway was reported to be faulty, and exactly a century later there was a Churrfield opening off Middle Street. Today the Cher runs from the end of Bampton Street to Hopcott Road.

Sir Hugh Luttrell I, like the last of the Mohuns, served valiantly in the wars against France. Possibly, however, he would have been content, once he had settled the question of his inheritance, to enjoy a quiet life in England; having been summoned back to active service in 1416 by Henry V, he was paid £286 the following year on condition that he served in person for 12 months, taking with him to France a force consisting of one knight, 19 esquires and 60 archers, most of whom must surely have been men of Dunster and Minehead. He took part in the siege of Rouen and, having been present at the taking of Harfleur in 1416, became its Governor. Finally he was Grand Seneschal of Normandy.

During his absences his wife, Lady Catherine, who bore him two sons and four daughters, saw to it that his affairs were well managed. When their eldest son, John, was old enough he acted as treasurer and overseer of the household accounts. His steward's accounts show how much was spent on fish, cheese, beans, wheat, oatmeal, malt and coal; how many oxen and sheep were bought for slaughter, and the quantity of salt obtained to preserve their meat. Robert Kynge of Minehead, shipman, transported cargoes of such goods to Harfleur for Sir Hugh and his men, and imported wine on his return voyages. This could be a profitable proceeding; when Sir Hugh sailed to Bordeaux in 1418, he did so in his own ship, the *Leonard*; the expenses of the voyage totalled just over £42, which was almost entirely met by the sale of wine brought back to England in the *Leonard*.

Although Sir Hugh was a man of considerable wealth, he appears to have run a fairly modest establishment at Dunster Castle; he had a chamberlain, a cook, 15 henchmen and servants and just one laundress. Lady Catherine had only one 'damsel' in attendance on her.

The household accounts refer to an upper and a lower castle. The former was the 'dongeon' or keep, which had in it the chapel of St Stephen built by the Mohuns, a kitchen and at least one tower. In the lower part were the main hall and rooms for the lord, the constable and the gatekeeper, two more towers and a second chapel.

Probably dissatisfied with the state of the castle as he found it – Lady Joan de Mohun, living far away in London or Canterbury, would have allowed it to become dilapidated – Sir Hugh spent about £252 between 1420 and 1424 on rebuilding work, including a splendid new gatehouse. He also built or restored a little chapel on the cliffs west of Minehead, the chapel of the Holy Trinity of Byrcombe, later to be known as the Burgundy Chapel. Its ruins may still be seen.[9]

In 1428 he died, and was buried 'in a manner befitting his rank' in Dunster church, where the effigies of himself and his wife, in alabaster, may still be seen. Unhappily that of Sir Hugh has been badly mutilated; only head and torso remain. His only surviving son, John, died two years later, leaving a three-year-

11. Weeding the corn, redrawn from the Luttrell Psalter (Traill and Mann).

old child, James, as his heir. A ward of Henry VI, James was brought up in the staunchly Lancastrian household of Sir Philip Courtenay; in his thirties he fought in the early battles of those civil wars between power-greedy barons that were later to be named, romantically, the Wars of the Roses. He died of wounds after the second Battle of St Albans, and was posthumously dispossessed of all his lands by the victorious Edward IV, who granted them in 1463 to William Herbert, Earl of Pembroke. After the earl's death his widow, and later his son, were permitted to hold them.

Yet for the tenants on the estates, the success of next year's harvest was probably of more importance than the identity of the great one – seldom or never seen – in whose manor court they were bound to do homage and where, if they misbehaved, they would be brought to account.

12. Gathering the harvest, redrawn from the Luttrell Psalter (Traill and Mann).

### Chapter Three

# *The People of a Medieval Manor:*
# *2. Deeds and Misdeeds*

In medieval England, all kinds of purposes useful to the lord of a manor were served in his manor court; the hearing of charges of misdemeanour was only one of them. The usual 'law days', on which courts were held, were at Hocktide (Hock Day was the second Tuesday after Easter Sunday) and Michaelmas. The lord's steward presided, the bailiff was required to be present (he would be fined for absenting himself) and there was a jury of 12 free men.

The lord's personal rules or ordinances – in effect a set of private bye-laws – would be made known. During the time when the widowed Countess of Pembroke was lady of Dunster and Minehead, in 1481, a set of such ordinances was issued in her manor court. According to these, tenants were forbidden to do certain things without special permission, such as setting up fish traps along the shore, or allowing anyone other than themselves to cultivate their holdings. No tenant or under-tenant was to keep any adulterous person in his house on pain of forfeiting his tenement. No man was unlawfully to play games after eight o'clock at night, or to carry arms, or to show a sign at his door and then refuse to sell beer. What is more, the Countess required a mid-winter wage freeze: 'no common labourer within the lordship shall take for his wage more than three-halfpence a day from the Feast of All Saints to the Feast of Purification' (1 November to 2 February).

The death of any tenant was reported at these courts, with the heriot to be paid to the lord: a sometimes harsh form of feudal death duty, when a widow's 'best beast' could be taken – a cow, an ox, a horse. From a poorer tenant, a pig might be demanded, or perhaps a bushel of barley or of salt. Ordinarily a widow was allowed to remain the tenant of her dead husband's holding, but she might not re-marry without the lord's consent. As late as 1565 a widow called Alice Gane was turned out of her Minehead tenement for marrying without permission since the previous court – and she still had to pay a sucking pig as heriot on the death of her former husband.

The threat of eviction was always held over the head of all tenants who might be tempted to behave in a way

13. Threshing, redrawn from the Luttrell Psalter (Traill and Mann).

14. The goose-herd, redrawn from the Luttrell Psalter (Traill and Mann).

displeasing to the lord. In 1481 a certain John Kelly was accused of unruly behaviour and removed from his tenancy; it was decreed that no one was to receive him within the lordship, on pain of a fine of 6s. 8d.

Local officials were elected at the courts. In Minehead, in the 14th century, two constables, two bread weighers (selling bread of short weight was a common offence) and two ale testers were appointed; a little later two surveyors of the shambles (the butchers' stalls or meat markets) were added, and by Tudor times, two keepers of the roads. Ale tasters were as important as bread weighers, at a time when, for country people, there was no other drink but water. There were many accusations of wrong-doing: selling ale without a sign, selling it in unmarked measures and giving short measure were the most usual. In the days of Joan de Mohun a certain Lucy Lyddon 'sold ale against the assize' and had three barrels confiscated 'to the use of the lady' (or, more probably, of the steward). The ale taster himself might not always give satisfaction: in 1507, for instance, one was fined sixpence because he 'did not behave well in executing his duty'.

One of the duties of the keeper of the roads was to see that 'the water' (the rivulet from Bratton) was not polluted or turned out of its course. Now and again whole groups of people were accused of offences of this kind. In 1507 seven men were fined for 'disturbing the course of the running water', and the whole tithing of the hamlet of Staunton was fined 'because the water at Fullebrigge has not been restrained to its proper course'; some half-century later two widows who had 'turned the water out of its proper course' were fined a shilling.

If any tenant had a complaint against one of his fellows, he had to bring it up in the lord's court; any attempt to prosecute the case outside the manor would bring down on him a large fine and, yet again, the probability of eviction. On at least one occasion, at Minehead, ill-feeling between neighbouring small-holders led to trespass on a *quid pro quo* basis: John Adam having earned a fine for depasturing his sheep in barley belonging to William Prikeprout, and his geese in Prikeprout's corn, the latter earned a similar fine for taking his pigs into Adam's beans and peas.

Over the centuries, the type of petty crime brought before the Minehead court did not vary much. Men might fight with fists, or knives, or swords (daggers and swords had to be confiscated, in accordance with the ordinance prohibiting the bearing of arms). Women might attack one another with domestic articles: 'Margaret Veale with one washyn ketyll assaulted Catherine Kyrie and drew her blood, fined sixpence'. There was even a charge of vicarious biting: Robert Bycombe was fined sixpence for a trespass against John Wood, 'viz., that with a certain dog he bit him'.

It was to the Manor Court that every tenant had to come to pay homage to his lord; omission of this duty meant a fine. It was also in the Manor Court that every tenant had to produce his copy of the entry in the Manor Court Roll relevant to his particular holding whenever it might be demanded. By the beginning of the 16th century the number of Minehead copyholders had hardly risen since the time of Sir Hugh Luttrell I. Holdings varied in size from a cottage to a farm of nearly seventy acres. Quite a few were split between moorland and what was termed Ryeland, on North Hill. There were eight boat houses, with a ninth in ruins.

As soon as the short-lived York line ended with the death of Richard III at Bosworth Field, Hugh Luttrell, the younger son of the ill-fated Sir James (the elder was dead), successfully petitioned Henry VII, in the first parliament after his accession, for the restitution of his lands, pleading that his father had forfeited them only through fighting loyally for his rightful sovereign. His request was granted. From 1485, Sir Hugh II and his descendants were to hold Dunster and Minehead in a firm grip for more than four centuries.

Even after the end of the Civil War, the authority of the Luttrells over the people of their manors seems to have hardly changed since the Middle Ages. Just as in 1380 some dozen men were fined for failing to do homage, so in 1655 William Fry and Hugh Trevelyan were said to owe 'free suit to this court' and were fined for defaulting; and as in earlier times no tenant might live outside his manor without licence (for instance, in 1582 Andrew Luttrell and Humphrey Wyndham, with seven others, were reported for this offence, and given until the next Feast of Pentecost to resume residence, on pain of a fine of 20 shillings) so in 1655 it was noted that a certain Alexander Lyne, and several others, did not make 'continuous abode upon his coppyhold tenement as by the customs of the same mannor he ought'. In far west Somerset, feudalism died hard.

15. A watermill, redrawn from the Luttrell Psalter (Traill and Mann).

16. A view in Dunster churchyard. After the Dissolution the Luttrells first leased and then bought all the former properties of the Priory; the priory church thus became their private property. Gradually, it seems, they neglected it. In the mid-18th century someone was paid a modest 5s. a year to clean the seats and monuments, but some forty years later Collinson saw it 'stript of all its furniture and totally neglected'. Forty years later again, Savage spoke of it in the same words, and wished that 'the voice of propriety and common decency ... would call upon the living to honour the remains of the illustrious dead'. At last, in 1875, George Luttrell called in an architect, J. C. Buckler, who carried out complete restoration at a cost of £12,000, of which Mr. Luttrell gave £10,000. It is one of the few contemporary works of the kind that seems not have attracted adverse criticism (Lyte).

17. The Priory dovecote, much visited in summer. It has been suggested that it was originally built by William de Mohun; certainly the Benedictine monks of Dunster Priory would have maintained it as a useful source of meat. The internal revolving ladder by means of which the nest holes were reached would still turn easily and silently – if it were not immobilised to prevent damage.

*Chapter Four*

# The People of a Medieval Parish

It seems that both Dunster and Minehead had churches in Saxon times. Their existence is indicated by a document issued by William de Mohun I. In 1090, wanting to have a new church for Dunster, he was able to give an existing one – probably small, and of timber – to the Abbey of Bath, together with half the tithes of a church existing in Minehead, as well as other tithes, lands and a tenth of his horses, in order that the monks of the Abbey should build a replacement. A small priory was set up to manage the church; apparently it never had more than half a dozen monks. For more than two centuries this cell remained wholly dependent on its parent abbey at Bath, but in 1332, when Robert de Sutton was appointed prior, it was granted a certain degree of independence.

It is ironic that one of the beauties of this particularly striking church remains to bear witness to a long-ago ecclesiastical squabble. This is the fan-vaulted oak rood screen of 14 arches, carved with vines and grapes and oak leaves. It commemorates a disagreement between the monks and the parishioners concerning their shared use of the church and payments expected for certain services. The parishioners evidently felt strongly about these matters; it seems that they, and not the monks, spent money on altering and rebuilding the church. In 1443, when the James Luttrell who was to die in the Lancastrian cause was a youth of only 17, they had been prosperous enough to commission James Marys of Stoke Courcy (Stogursey) to build a new tower for it. Marys built them a 90-foot tower; they supplied tools and materials, and paid him 13s. 4d. a foot.[1]

When disagreements with the monks came to a head, the whole question was referred to the Bishop, who appointed three arbitrators, headed by the Abbot of Glastonbury. The decision reached was that in future the church should be divided; the monks might use the part east of the tower and the vicar and parishioners the nave. An agreement to this effect was signed by the Prior and Convent of Bath, the Prior and Convent of Dunster, the vicar of Dunster, Sir Hugh Luttrell II and the parishioners. The screen was erected to mark the division.

The eastern part of the church, restored by J. C. Buckler in the 1870s at a cost of £12,000 – largely paid by George Luttrell – contains one tomb that has been dated to about 1315 and said to be that of a lady of the Mohun family.[2] Her effigy and the canopy over it are of stone from Ham Hill in south Somerset. She lies with her feet on a long-eared dog. The effigies of Sir Hugh Luttrell I and his wife, already referred to, lie on their tomb chests in a recess near the chantry chapel of St Lawrence. Let into the floor is an alabaster slab depicting Sir Hugh's mother, Lady Elizabeth, the purchaser of the Luttrell estates. She wears an ermine-faced gown and long mantle; a veil covers her head and falls to her shoulders. This stone has been moved; when

18. This beautiful fan-vaulted rood screen remains as a memorial to a 15th-century squabble between the monks of Dunster Priory and the parishioners over their shared use of the church: it marks the division finally agreed (Lyte).

19. The High House, Dunster. Although this house bears the name 'The Nunnery' on its door, writers on Dunster have repeatedly pointed out that there is no record that it has ever been a nunnery (Lyte).

20. The shouldered arch in the south transept of Dunster church. Pevsner suggests that this a Late Perpendicular adjustment.

21. St Michael's church, Minehead, at the beginning of the 20th century. Externally, it would have looked much as it does here from the time its tower was completed in the 15th century.

she died in 1395 she was buried before the high altar. Later Luttrell tombs, large and ornate, are those of a 16th-century Thomas Luttrell, his son George and their wives.[3]

William de Mohun IV[4] gave the advowson, the remainder of the tithes of Minehead and 'much land' to the Augustinian monastery of Bruton, some nine miles south-east of Shepton Mallet. The Prior of Bruton presented vicars to the living of Minehead until the late 15th century.[5]

Little remains of the building they served; Dr. Eeles, in his book on the church, suggests that 'the present nave wall may contain a certain amount of Norman or early English work. But no detail earlier than the 14th century is visible'. The porch and south doorway, he says, 'represent the earliest untouched portions of the building, though there is probably a good deal more 14th century work in the walls'. The arcade, which may have been built about the end of the 14th century, does indicate that the aisle was added to an earlier church. If this dating is correct, the addition was made at about the time when the widowed Joan de Mohun held the manor, and Mattheus Eliot was vicar, officially, despite the mysterious references to the agricultural Adam, already mentioned.

The town must have been relatively prosperous, in spite of the presumed toll of that terrible half-century of plague outbreaks, to undertake the building, or rebuilding, of a church of the size we see today, although the splendid 87-foot tower of pale silvery-green limestone did not rise until about a century after the main structure. The church's patron saint, St Michael, appears on the east face of the tower, weighing souls; a small vicious cat-like devil tugs in vain at the scales while the Virgin Mary calmly presses on the balance.

From 1484 until 1497 the vicar was Richard FitzJames, who later held the bishoprics of Rochester, Chichester and finally of London. As a cleric who held positions at the courts of Edward IV and Henry VII, he may have been influential enough to obtain financial help in the building of the tower. Today, his beautifully illuminated missal and the excellently preserved hutch-chest with delicate carving which he gave to the church are among the treasures to be seen in St Michael's.

In any medieval church, many lights burned perpetually. There was the devotion or dead light, the rood light, the High Cross light, a light dedicated to the patron saint of the church and possibly lights dedicated to other saints. The faithful left money to maintain such lights. In 1502 George Dovell left twopence to each light of Minehead church and 6s. 8d. to the church itself; seven years later John Butston of Minehead left fourpence to each of the lights, and also 'half the ship which is called *Puppis* to a priest to celebrate for one year for me and my friends'; in 1530 John Dalon left fourpence to each of six lights, including one to Our Lady of Pity and another to St Erasmus, one of the patron saints of sailors. It is thought that there may have been a chapel or chantry for a sailors' guild in the chancel at one time; outside the east window of the north aisle is an inscription 'We prey to Jesu and Marie to send our neyburs safete'.

As early as 1417 a former vicar of the parish, Richard Bruton, left ten shillings 'to the parish church of Mynhed to mend their glass windows'. Bequests for the repair and upkeep of the church were numerous: a merchant in 1513 left a small sum 'to the werks of the body of the same', and a ship-owner left 'a quarter of my vessel called the *Patrik*'. Some people left animals for its maintenance: a cow, thirty sheep, even a barrel of herrings. Dunster parishioners made similar bequests to the lights of their church of St George and to its fabric. At the beginning of the 16th century the aisle of the Holy Trinity at Dunster was either in need of repair or being rebuilt: a merchant left ten tons of iron 'coming in a ship of John Cokkys' on condition that a start was made on the aisle within three years, and some time later a widow left the modest sum of twenty pence to the same cause.[6]

Although Minehead's register of burials begins in 1548, its registers of baptisms and marriages do not begin until October 1559. Leland, in the 1540s, found the town full of Irishmen, but they must have been Irish sailors, not residents; the 16th-century registers show hardly any Irish surnames, although Welsh ones are numerous: Morgan, Owen, Davies, Gryffeths, Jenckyns, Williams, Welshe, Jones and so on.

As is to be expected, not a few burials are of men, and sometimes women, drowned off the coast. In 1588, John and Edward Saise 'with divers others cast awie with the bote of Newton without the key' were buried; ten years later six men were buried on Michaelmas day, having been cast away 'at the Ridges out of a Barke of Gersey of whom one was an Irish merchant'. In 1617 eight 'strange' were lost in the wreck of a Bristol ship: five men and three women. 'The chiefest of the women found and buried was one Mrs. Margt. Goldwell a Londin' [sic]. There was also Mrs. Johnson, wife of the Controller of Cork. Beggars, unnamed strangers and soldiers come from Ireland and die; passengers bound for Ireland fall ill and die while waiting for a ship; vessels put in from Devon or Lundy or Wales with dead sailors aboard, and all find their graves in the churchyard of Minehead.

A surname that soon begins to appear frequently in the registers is that of the Quirkes, a family which was locally influential for more than two centuries. In 1472 a John Quirke is recorded as failing to answer a summons for debt, but by 1498 a Morys Quirke is one of the 'honest men sworne, both maisters and maryners of shippes and vesselles' in an Admiralty Court held by Sir Hugh Luttrell II. In 1505 a Robert Quirke is found in the rent roll of the manor, and several Quirkes, variously spelled, are included in the subsidy rolls of the early 16th century: in 1523 a Robert Quyrke pays 11 shillings on goods valued at £11, which makes him one of the most substantial townspeople of his time. It was perhaps his widow Joanna who had to pay nearly 25 shillings on goods worth £26 in 1546. When Elizabeth I granted the borough its charter in 1558, a Robert Quirke was one of the first principal burgesses chosen, and in 1565 a report to the queen concerning the port of Bridgwater recorded that Robert Quyrke was deputy to the customs officer.

In 1600 a James Quirke took a water mill and a water course, for a term of 99 years, from George Luttrell, at a rent of 10 shillings. This may be the same James Quirke who died in 1613 and whose memorial describes him as a mariner who had 'purchased the fee farm of the moytee of this rectorie'. He was in fact a merchant, and represented Minehead in the parliament of 1592-3.

But it was Robert Quirke, baptised in 1583, who has left his memorial both in the church and in the town; he was named by Thomas Wyndham, in a will leaving a sum of money 'to the poore of the towne of Minehead for ever', as one of the six most honest and substantial men of the town.

22. Robert Quirke's Almshouses, Minehead (Spranklin; Preb. Hancock).

23. The Quirke alsmhouses in Market House Lane, Minehead, as they were in 1984, immediately before restoration work began. Their forlorn appearance may be contrasted with Spranklin's perhaps idealised drawing of the houses in Edwardian days. By the beginning of 1987 they had been re-roofed, and interior work was almost complete.

On the north wall of the church are two large painted panels, flanked by almost life-sized figures representing Moses and Aaron. These once hung behind the altar. Inscribed on them are the Creed and the Commandments, with the information that 'Robert Quirke, the Younger, Mariner, Sonne of James Quirke, gave this to the church, Anno Domini 1634'.

As one of the freeholders of the manor of Minehead, Quirke rented 'one plot or piece of waste land' from Francis Luttrell, with the intention of building an almshouse. The plot lay near the cross in the Old Market Place; it measured about 114 feet by 16 feet, and on it Robert Quirke built 11 dwellings 'for the relief, succour and comfort of the distressed, impotent, poor persons of the said parish of Minehead'. On one cottage is a brass plate which bears an engraving of a three-masted ship and the inscription:

ROBERT QVRKE SONNE OF JAMES QVRKE
BUILT THIS HOUSE ANO : 1630 : AND
DOTH GIVE IT TO THE USE OF THE
POORE OF THIS PARISH FOR EVER AND FOR
BETTER MAINTENANCE DOE GIVE MY TWO
INNER SELLERS AT THE INNER END OF THE
KEY AND CURSED BEE THAT MAN THAT SHALL
CONVERT IT TO ANY OTHER VSE THAN TO
THE VSE OF THE POORE 1630
GOD'S PROVIDENCE
IS MY INHERITANCE
R.   Q.
E.

While restoration work was being carried out the brass place was removed, but is now back in place. He also rented a plot of waste land on the west side of the harbour 'upon the beach of Chezell'. (The word *chezell* or *chesil*, as at Chesil Bank, means a pebbled shore.) On this he built a cellar or store house, and in his will, dated 1648, he directed that his 'two inner cellars at the key of Minehead' should be let out for rent 'to him that will give the most money for them', and the money used for the upkeep of the almshouses, any sums remaining being divided among their occupants.

The following year he died. His name and that of his father are inscribed on a slab of stone set into the floor of the chancel. There is also a fine slab of blue marble (protected today by a carpet) which bears a brass depicting a young woman in 15th-century dress. Somehow the Quirkes appropriated it as a memorial to several members of their family, the last being to Alice, who died in 1700 at the age of seventy-five. Other Quirke monuments may be seen in the church, including a stone in the nave to Isott Quirke who died in 1768 at the age of ninety.

The beneficent 17th-century Robert Quirke was a churchwarden. As such, he signed the Terrier of Minehead glebe lands in 1633. The document shows that the total extent of the glebe was about thirty-two acres, including five 'closes' of between two and five acres and nine tenements with gardens. They all lay in a circle around the vicarage, with the exception of a five-acre close about a quarter of a mile to the west. All tenants – of whom four were widows – held their tenements 'according to the Antient Customs of the Mannor of Minehead'. Those who held only a house and garden paid rents of four or five shillings a year; but, like other parishioners, they had to pay tithes. Throughout the parish the tenth of wool, apples, corn and hops went to the vicar, as did the tenth cock of hay except on the demesne, where half the tithe hay went to Dunster church and half to Minehead. Roasting pigs were tithable as soon as they were 18 days old; if the owner had seven in a litter, he had to give one to the vicar, who would give him three-halfpence for it. The payment of tithes was apt to be resented, and it would seem that tithe evasion was as prevalent in late-medieval times as tax evasion is today. Again and again, in contemporary wills, an item appears leaving a certain sum – not, usually, a very large one – for 'tithes forgotten' or more honestly 'tithes with-holden'.

Certain other dues and obligations were laid down; every householder was expected to pay twopence at Easter on behalf of himself, his wife, children and apprentices who were communicants. Servants of both sexes also had to give twopence and, for their private tithes, menservants paid fourpence and maidservants threepence. At Easter anyone who owned a newly-calved cow had to pay fourpence – twopence for the calf, twopence for the milk. There was, moreover, a court which the vicar might call as and when he pleased; his own tenants had to do suit at it or pay a fine.

Among the details of the glebe lands is one especially interesting piece of ground: a hemp garden, divided among several tenants. In the days of self-sufficiency it was natural for a seaport to make its own rope for shipping; Minehead also grew the raw material, and may have continued to do so well into the 18th century, when a serge-maker called John Bowden held, by copy of the vicarage court roll, a cottage and garden with 'three other gardens called the Hemp Gardens'. Today there still exists a short street called Hemp Gardens running from Vicarage Road, below the parish church, to Watery Lane.

*Chapter Five*

# The Harbours of Dunster and Minehead

As early as the 12th century, the mouth of the little river Avill provided Dunster with a pill or creek where the small ships of the period could berth. It is known that Dunster's reeve was making himself some money on the side by illegally importing corn there in 1183. His venture can hardly have been profitable, as he was convicted and fined more than five pounds. In the time of the John de Mohun who inherited in 1279, there is mention in a deed of 'the road which leads to the sea port of Dunster'. A remnant of the vanished harbour may be seen today in a long narrow pool a few hundred yards north of Dunster station, lying parallel with the shore. It is quite big enough, were it not land-locked, to accommodate two or three sailing coasters of the Middle Ages, and is marked on modern Ordnance maps as the Hawn, a name that occurs in Elizabethan documents and may be a corruption of *haven*. In the 19th century it was called the Hone.

At intervals during the various wars with France between the late 13th and early 15th centuries, orders were issued to arrest shipping in English harbours for the king's use. Dunster, with Bridgwater, was more than once included in these embargoes. By contrast, in 1338, Dunster was the only port in Somerset, apart from Bridgwater, to which, it was proclaimed, merchants from Gascony, Italy and Spain might come to trade in safety. Later in that century, however, Richard II had to direct that redoubtable lady, Joan de Mohun, to restore to two Genoese ship-owners the goods that her agent had seized from their ship which, badly off course, had been driven into Dunster Haven. It had been carrying a rich and varied cargo from Genoa to Sluys: raisins, cinnamon, pepper, white sugar, ginger 'green and cured with lemon juice', prunes, sulphur, woad, flax and writing paper.[1]

In 1561 Thomas Luttrell of Dunster Castle had a dispute with the portreeve and burgesses of Minehead because they had been taking weirage duties from ships bound for Dunster Haven. Three years later a royal commission described Dunster as a place where 'small botes' could bring in such commodities as wine, salt, coal, timber and wool. Most of the wool came from Wales, often in Welsh ships, although in 1566, for instance, the *Michael* of Dunster carried a hundred stones of it from Milford Haven.[2]

Thomas Gerard, who published his *Particular Description of Somerset* in 1633, saw Dunster as 'A little Markett Towne seated on a flatt altogether environed with hills except towards ye Sea ... often visited by such as passe to and from Irland, for that in the mouth of this River ... there is a pretty harbour'.

Even in the 1640s Dunster Haven was still in use; there is a record of the *Gift* of Swansea paying fourpence in keelage duty at Minehead on her way to Dunster during the Civil War.[3] From that time the little creek must have gradually silted up. In any case, Minehead's harbour had long since overtaken Dunster's in importance. Some kind of landing stage or small pier must have been in existence by the 14th century, and probably earlier, since weirage duties (harbour dues) were being collected for the maintenance of the port and harbour when the last John de Mohun was lord of the manor.

Once the Luttrells took over, they began the record of pier-building that was to go on for centuries. In 1421 Lady Margaret Luttrell, daughter-in-law of Sir Hugh I, gave her Minehead tenants ten shillings towards making a *juttee* (the Middle English form of jetty) which was often referred to as 'le weir'. During the years when, by favour of Edward IV, Dunster and Minehead were in the hands of the Earl of Pembroke, the bailiffs included in their accounts 20 shillings 'lately coming of the toll and custom of the sea', adding that 'There is nothing this year, because it has been given to the tenants of the town, for the maintenance of the weir at the lord's will'.

During those years, Minehead was the only port in Somerset permitted to engage in the pilgrim trade; possibly the Earl's influence ensured this. In the late 14th century and during the 15th, large numbers of pilgrims were drawn to make a voyage to visit the shrine of St James of Compostella in Spain. Some ship-owners, having obtained the necessary licence for this passenger traffic, made considerable profits out of the pilgrims, many of whom endured acute discomforts in the small, overcrowded ships.

Possibly the Earl, as an absentee landlord, did little to ensure the upkeep of the jetty. Certainly when Sir Hugh Luttrell II regained the family estates in 1485, he evidently considered it inadequate. According to a document of the early 18th century outlining the Luttrell's version of the history of the harbour, he first built a small pier, and then 'much enlarged it, which made the harbour considerable, and did encourage ships to harbour there, which in a few years ... inriched the inhabitants'. It also helped to enrich the royal exchequer; Sir Hugh's steward at Minehead, John Dobyll, included in his records for 1491 a receipt for £5 for 'ye profitts of ye king's customers of Minehead according to ye king's command'.

Sir Hugh II, like many of his predecessors, was often absent on military service, but he held the office of Vice-Admiral of Minehead. This was not a naval appointment. There were 19 vice-admiralties, one for each of the maritime counties of England, with jurisdiction over all matters concerning rivers, shores and sea ports; each vice-admiral held an annual court 'where every man's complaint may be publicly heard'.

One case heard by Sir Hugh was the complaint of a William Kyste of Swansea against Robert Bassher of Minehead, in 1498. Bassher had rented from Kyste a type of small ship called a pickard for a fishing voyage. The vessel had been seized during the war between Henry VII and James IV of Scotland. Bassher had ransomed it, and then tried to hold on to it; Kyste was suing to reclaim it. The 'twelve honest men sworn' – all masters or mariners of Minehead – found for Kyste, declaring that Bassher should pay one-seventh of the value of fish caught, and one-fourth of any freight, as had been agreed between the two men, and return the pickard to Kyste, who in turn was to pay a sixth of the ransom. Bassher ignored the court's decision and Kyste's further attempts to get his ship back. It seems strange that Sir Hugh did not simply order it to be impounded and given into Kyste's hands. The final result is not known, although Kyste obtained a writ of privy seal and Bassher was ordered to appear before the Star Chamber.

In Tudor times, merchants and ship-owners often left money to the upkeep of the weir, or pier; for instance Thomas Braye, in 1513, left 10 shillings; Robert Burke, in 1523, left 20 shillings 'to the reparacion and amendment of the were of Mynnet'; Thomas Cole, in 1526, left 20 shillings 'to the store of the port called le Were'.[4]

At the beginning of Elizabeth I's reign the people of Minehead claimed that a pier or quay had been maintained at a yearly charge of £50 or more 'against the greate sea time out of mind'. But because of 'sundrie warres' shipping, and therefore customs dues, were reduced, and so the pier had fallen into decay. If it was not repaired before the next summer, they said, piling it on in the style customary at the period when asking for royal assistance, 'no shippe nor bote can take succour there to the great annoyance of that west partys of Somerset, Devonscheir and Cornewall'. The ancient and daily passage of trade from Glamorgan, by means of which 'the faires and markets of your countie aforesaid have ever been furnished with no small number of cattle, shepe, woole, yarne, clothe, butter, stone (limestone to be burned), coal, oysteres, salmon and other sundrie kinds of fish and flesh' would be halted 'to the losses of your majestys customs there'. There would be 'dystrokssyon' of ships in stormy weather, and moreover 'dysplassing of our honoryd seafaring poor men from their houses to seeke they know not where; the utter undowing of your saide toune unless that your Highness of your most gracious pitie and clemencie doe extend unto them and their successors for their comffort and better maintenaynce of the same Pyer your most gracious grawnnte of a Borowe Port Reve and Burgessys'.

Although the Privy Council at first expressed some doubt that as much as £50 a year had been spent on the pier, a charter was granted to Minehead in the first year of Elizabeth's reign, 1558. It conceded that revenue on imports and exports had been almost destroyed by recent wars, and that the port was going to ruin, so that no ship of burden, not even the smallest skiff, could anchor in it safely. More importantly, it acknowledged that the Crown would lose its port dues and customs if things were not improved.

Minehead was therefore constituted 'a free borough incorporate under the name of the Port Reeve and Burgesses of the same borough'. The corporation was to have the usual powers to hold property, to grant leases, bring and defend actions and make ordinances for the good government of the townspeople, and also to ensure the proper victualling of the borough. The first man to hold the office of portreeve was John Dodinge; 12 capital burgesses were appointed to assist him.

The portreeve and burgesses had the power to choose 'a fit and worthy man learned in the laws of England' to be Sergeant at Mace; his duties included making proclamations, arrests and processes. Wrong-doers brought before the steward in his Court of Record, where cases of a value of up to £40 might be heard, could possibly end up in the borough's newly-granted prison. There was in addition a court of pie powder, that medieval institution, in connection with the weekly Thursday market and the two annual fairs, one on 1 March, the other on 23 June, both to continue until noon on the following day. All money arising from fines in the court of pie powder and all dues deriving from the markets and fairs were to be used for 'the proper behoof use and utility of the portreeve and burgesses'. People could only sell from ships by licence of the corporation. As was usual, the burgesses themselves were free of all tolls, passage, stallage, picage and so on, throughout the realm.

There was one very important proviso: the charter was to be forfeited if the port, which in effect meant the pier or quay, was not kept up. Having defied the Luttrells by petitioning for a charter it seems that within a few years the townspeople were beginning to feel that they had bitten off more than they could chew in assuming responsibility for the harbour facilities. In 1564, only six years after the charter had been granted, they were seeking the help of Thomas Luttrell, a grandson of Sir Hugh II, to repair the quay. Mr. Luttrell evidently decided to let them get on with it and see how they liked it. A letter from Robert Quirke on behalf of himself and other burgesses declaring that they 'accepted Mr. Lutrell as prinsypall burgess within his towne of Mynhed' would have cut no ice at all: he knew very well who he was, lord of both Minehead and Dunster. Moreover, he had taken the opportunity of becoming one of Minehead's two representatives in parliament, a Thomas Fitzwilliams being his fellow M.P.

It was in the year after this unsuccessful appeal that the Queen sent a commission to Bridgwater 'to examine all the creeks and ports thereto adjoining' and report to the Barons of the Exchequer. Minehead, they duly reported, belonged to the port of Bridgwater; it was haunted by vessels bringing in victuals, salt, wine, coal and wood, but little other merchandise. The 'creek' of Minehead was decayed by a parocke (a medieval word for an enclosure; in *Piers Plowman* Wrath is described as 'y-parocked in a pew' among squabbling women) which the inhabitants were bound by their charter to work on yearly. This enclosure was the bank of stones that was repeatedly washed up by the tides to block the harbour bed.

The customs controller of Bridgwater had a deputy at Minehead 'and so have had tyme out of mynd and do and have always taken entries ther to the inwards and outwards'. At this time Robert Quirke was the deputy; like his predecessors, he hired a house for an annual rent of 6s. 8d., though he claimed to receive no allowance for this.

It seems that Thomas Luttrell gradually came round to the idea that he would have to help the people of Minehead to repair their pier, and in 1570, a year before his death, he sent out an appeal for funds. He had undertaken, he said, 'to my great charge with some assistance of my good and well-willing tenants to make a new key or Piere at Mynehed as a harbour for shipping'. He was determined to make it 'such a harbour as never was beleek ... in the west part of England'; it would enrich Minehead and the country around, and also provide a safe refuge for 'all shippinge passing in and out of Severan'. But it would be costly and needed the help of 'my good neighbours friends and well-willers who may and shall be partakers of ye great commoditie'.

Sending out collectors with copies of his letter, he asked each 'well-willer' to signify what he was willing to give. As a result, according to a document of the time of his son George, towards the end of Elizabeth's reign, the sum of £200 was collected from his friends and tenants. This document contends that Minehead had been better governed before it received its charter of incorporation: 'the magistrates and burgesses of whom the corporation consists are but simple and rude handicraftsmen who are fitter to be governed than to govern others ... by their misgovernment there have been many affrays in the town, and some murders in Dunster'. There were too many licensed 'tiplers' or small ale houses, the town was depopulated, the weekly market decayed, and there were only five or six boats in the harbour instead of thirty or forty.

George Luttrell explained that he had begun to build a new quay about three hundred paces from the earlier one, putting up £600 of his own money, but needed at least another thousand pounds. When the harbour was finished it would take 'Her Majesty's ships' and be the fittest in all the west for transporting soldiers, munitions and victuals to Ireland, as well as being a useful *entrepôt* between Wales and the south-western counties. Moreover, gains from customs dues would be increased.

It is probable that from the time of Thomas Luttrell's death in 1571 little had been done in the way of pier-building because of the diversion of money, men and effort to defence needs. In 1570 there was a general arrest of shipping for the Queen's service; surprisingly, it was reported that there were only two ships in Minehead harbour, the *Margett* of 35 tons burden and the *Saviour* of 46 tons, and 'no more shippes nor barkes in that port neither at home nor abroad'. There were only five seamen, including John, one of the Quirke family, on shore. 'The residue of the mariners of this porte be also in the service of the quenes Highnes and at sea in other small vessels of that porte'.

Although the Luttrells were to claim, more than a century later, that Minehead harbour had been useless, except for fishermen, during the remainder of Elizabeth's reign, a certain amount of trade went on, chiefly the importation of wool from Wales. Contemporary Welsh port books give the names of some of the very small vessels carrying cargoes from Tenby, Milford and Cardiff to Minehead. A few of the ships are given as 'of Minehead': there is *Le Ffog de Myned* of 16 tons, *Le Cheribim de Mynet*

| Bridgwater | Watchet | Minehead ('Mynyad') | Porlock |

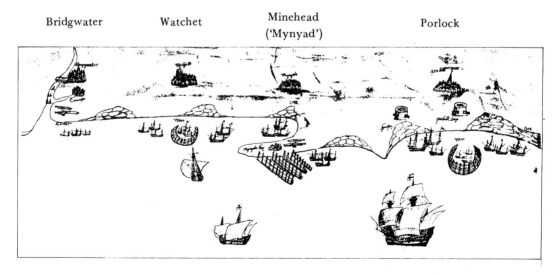

24. Fortifications at Watchet, Minehead and Porlock: part of a map attributed to the time of Henry VIII (Green).

of 12 tons and *Le Trinitie de Myned* of 20 tons. The weight of their cargoes of wool is given in stones, and usually amounts to between 300 and 700 stones. These were apparently stones of 18 pounds, not 14, so 500 stones, say, would have amounted to just over four tons.[5]

During the years immediately before the Armada, there was presumably virtually no trade at all from the port, since the only ships available were held for possible use against Spain. Like every maritime county, Somerset was on the alert; in October 1586 it was reported that watch had been set in every town, the beacons were ready and guarded and searches for suspicious persons were carried out. Coastal defences included the erection of towers armed with cannon at Porlock, Hurlstone and Uphill, and the provision of guns of some kind at Minehead. In March 1588, a few months before the Armada sailed, the Muster Master of Somerset, Captain Ourd, found the county's defenders brave and well supplied with arms. 'It is a most gallant country for men, armour, and readiness, and they may well guard Her Majesty's person', he reported.

However, a few years after those alarms were at an end, a copy of the weirage duties, or harbour dues, of Minehead was included among the Dunster Castle records, taken from 'a certain table which did hange in the Comon Hall to be seen of all'. These dues, which it was claimed had been paid time out of mind, included a penny on every pack of wool or yarn, and a further halfpenny for weighing every stone of wool, which meant that on the above-mentioned 500-stone cargo a duty of more than twenty shillings was payable to the Luttrells as lords of the manor, merely for the use of their weighing beam; a surprisingly high impost. Other charges were a shilling for a cargo of white fish, a penny a barrel on herrings, fourpence on a tun of wine from Spain and sixpence on a tun of wine from France. A tun of 'trayne' or whale oil paid sixpence, but a barrel of tar was only a penny, as was a barrel of butter or a 'hundred' of 'Sope, Mather or Alum'.

In view of the money to be made from the wool trade alone, it is not to be wondered at that the Luttrells wanted to ensure that they, and not the burgesses, held the harbour. Eventually, they had their way. A new enquiry into the state of the port was requested by the Exchequer late in Elizabeth's reign; the jurors or witnesses − 17 of them in all − stated that for the past 20 years the bailiffs and burgesses of the borough of Minehead had failed to repair and maintain the harbour, which was obstructed and choked with sand and stones, so that ships large and small were in danger of being wrecked if they called there. The Queen did not act on this report, but James I, not long after his accession, revoked the borough's charter. George Luttrell, still lord of the manor, no doubt received the news with great satisfaction.

George Luttrell lived a longer life than any of his ancestors in the direct line for many generations; he was 69 when he died. Although Sir Hugh I survived into his sixties, despite his busy military career, the 15th and 16th centuries saw at least five of the male members of the family who held Dunster Castle dying in their thirties or forties. The most interesting of all was perhaps the Sir John Luttrell who was born in 1519. If the remarkable and complex allegorical portrait of him which may still be seen in the castle is a good likeness, he was a handsome man. He fought with vigour in Henry VIII's Scottish wars, leading 300 men in the vanguard of the English army at the battle of Pinkie. In 1545 he was captain of the *Mary of Hambrough*, of 400 tons, which carried 240 men and was said to be in the vanguard of the king's navy 'towards the Narro Sees, wher, as it apperith, the Frenchmen doo tryumphe'.[6] (Two Minehead ships were requisitioned to join this fleet, the *Saviour* of 65 tons and the *Tawderey* of 30 tons.) When Sir John died, of the 'sweating sickness', at the early age of 32, he was planning an expedition to Morocco. Edward VI had granted him 100 marks a year for life, but he spent money freely.[7] He evidently did run into debt; not long before he died he mortgaged Minehead Park to his cousin Hugh Stewkeley, a lawyer, for £230. His brother Thomas, having inherited, outlived him for 20 years, yet was only 46 when he died, leaving his 10-year-old son George as his heir.

Hugh Stewkeley, who had a house at Marsh, just north of Dunster, became George's guardian. Here once again appears the theme of ward marrying guardian's daughter: when George Luttrell was 15 he became engaged to

25. Sir John Luttrell, *c.*1519-1551. This line drawing is based on the original painting to be seen in Dunster Castle (Lyte).

Stewkeley's daughter Joan. From that time he referred to himself as her husband, and addressed her parents as 'mother' and 'father'. The Luttrell family opposed the match; in their opinion Stewkeley was a 'miseree' and Joan a slut. George was sent to Cambridge. Having graduated, he married Joan in 1580.

Several of his father's relations held parts of the Luttrell estates as jointures. As, one by one, they died, George grew more prosperous. Much of his money was spent on buildings of one kind and another. There was the long-projected pier at Minehead, 'not on the same place where the former stood, but in a much more advantageous place'; it cost him £5,000, far more than he had originally estimated, but it provided a greatly enlarged harbour.

When Joan died, George married again, in his sixties; for his apparently far from amiable second wife, Sylvestra, he altered and enlarged the Luttrell house at East Quantoxhead which several of his ancestors and descendants, women especially, preferred to Dunster Castle as a dwelling. In 1617 he embarked on his most ambitious project of all: he commissioned the building of a splendid new house inside the ancient fortifications of the castle. His architect was William Arnold, with whom he fell out over money, but not before Arnold had designed a house having the H-shaped ground plan characteristic of the period, ornamented with three towers and walls topped by battlements. Externally, at least, the house was to remain largely unaltered for 250 years; it is shown in various engravings and water colours of the 18th and early 19th centuries.

Only the outer defences remained to remind the Luttrells of their medieval past – yet in just over a dozen years after George Luttrell's death, those defences were to withstand their fiercest test since the second William de Mohun had defied King Stephen.

North west front of
Dunster Castle. 1868.
F.F. Lyte del.

26. For some 250 years after George Luttrell had ordered it to be built, his castle-house was little changed, externally, except for the addition of a chapel on the south-east side by Dorothy Luttrell in 1722. Thus the men who arrived in 1649 with orders from Cromwell to destroy it would have seen it looking much as it appears in this drawing made by F. F. Lyte in 1868, immediately before Salvin began his reconstruction. They had slighted the defensive walls and were ready to begin on the house itself when, for some unknown but fortunate reason, the Council of State had second thoughts. George Luttrell paid a large recognisance, swore allegiance to the Commonwealth and was appointed Sheriff of Somerset.

*Chapter Six*

# Troubles at Sea, Conflicts on Land

From the time of the Viking raids, places on the shores of the Severn Sea were liable to attack by ship-borne forces of one kind and another. In the reign of Edward III, various sea-raiders were so ill-advised as to plunder ships carrying provisions to the king in Gascony, as well as harrying people ashore. Edward sent orders that this 'body of evil-doers' was to be caught and punished, to prevent further intolerable mischief being done to his kingdom 'especially during our absence in France'. This particular pirate group was said to be made up of men from the Somerset and Gloucestershire coasts (the Gloucestershire men presumably coming from the Severn shore) and to have its headquarters in Bristol, but it is not impossible that a few Minehead mariners joined it.

In Tudor times, acts of piracy were increasingly international. The crew of a ship sailing from Bristol in Henry VIII's time was seized by Spaniards, who accused them of piracy and handed them over to the Inquisition, which was tantamount to a death penalty; the reported plight of the wives and children moved the Privy Council to pity. But when, three years later, some 'men of Mynet' were charged with depredations done upon a Breton ship, Thomas Cromwell, the king's minister, investigated the case; the guilty seamen were imprisoned, and Cromwell directed that they should be 'sent for to make satisfaction to the king for the money paid to the Breton for the piracy'.

A number of Minehead men are known to have sailed on unlawful voyages during these years. They made attacks on Portuguese ships, bringing back cargoes of such things as rice, almonds and treacle. On one occasion Sir John Luttrell was ordered to see to it that Thomas Wyndham returned two bags of pepper, then a commodity of considerable value, to their Portuguese owner.

In fact piracy was so rampant that troop transports returning from delivering a detachment of soldiers to Ireland were told to search the Bristol Channel coast for privateers. In Edward VI's reign a certain Robert Cole of Minehead confessed to having been a pirate for a year, and to have captured 'divers prizes', but at the same time claimed that he deserved to be pardoned, for he had taken an Irish castle at the bidding of the Lord Deputy of Ireland.

During these years around the middle of the 16th century, Minehead apparently possessed several ships of some size. There was a 70-ton vessel with four guns belonging to William Hill, two of 60 tons belonging to Robert Quirke and Denys Marrane, and one of 100 tons belonging to Lady Luttrell. Yet, as has been said, only two were reported in the harbour in 1570, and two years later, when Thomas Colshill, surveyor of the customs in the port of London, compiled his register of coasting vessels, there were still only two, and these were very small indeed, one of 30 tons and the other a mere ten.[1]

For all that, in the 1570s domestic piracy was still going on; Elizabeth commanded the Commissioners in Somerset to enquire into the activities of those who in the five years since 1572 had 'set forth shippes to the seas in warlike sort', as well as those who had been 'favourers and assisters of pirates, buyers, receivers or conveyors of pirate goods'. The Commissioners seem to have had little success; in the Minehead area their only arrest was of a John Overs of Dunster, charged with buying molasses from a man who was known to be a pirate. Elizabeth was not at all averse to piracy of another kind – attacks on merchant and treasure ships belonging to Spain; she willingly issued letters of marque to captains capable of sailing out on such voyages. However, it is possible that during her reign Minehead never possessed any vessel large enough, or captain bold enough, to apply for such a licence.

Early in James I's reign Lundy, as often before, became a refuge for lawless men who, under their leader Thomas Salkeld, sailed the Severn Sea and attacked shipping, including, probably, coasters from Minehead, until he was arrested and taken to Pembrokeshire for trial. Charles I, like Elizabeth, was prepared to issue letters of marque; among the recipients in 1627 were Captain Thomas Lee and Hugh Davis of Minehead. They owned jointly two ships, the *Elizabeth* of Minehead of 60 tons and the *James* of Minehead, 30 tons.

It was a reciprocal trade; Spanish, French and Dutch privateers seized English vessels. Minehead became so alarmed at the dangers to her trade with Ireland and even Wales that she petitioned to be allowed to provide and arm a ship to act as a guard. When permission was granted, the *Dove*, an 80-ton vessel belonging to a Henry Powlett, was chosen. It was captained by a Henry Hastings, who had experience of the privateering business. He captured a Spanish ship in the Bay of Biscay in 1630, and sought permission to bring her into Minehead; she was laden with pitch and rosin. Two other prizes he brought in contained pitch, as well as pipe staves, whale oil, beeswax, knives, iron pots and 'Normandy cloth and coloured stuffs and white stuff'.

With the *Dove*, Hastings captured a Portuguese prize. Somewhat surprisingly, he made for the Azores with her cargo of ambergris, tobacco, oil, salt and fish – whereupon a Dutchman, Cornelius Kint, captured the *Dove* and took her back to Madeira where her crew, many of them dangerously wounded, were thrown into prison. For years afterwards Robert Powlett, perhaps a brother of the *Dove*'s owner and 'sometime customer [customs officer] of Bridgwater and Minehead', was complaining to the Lord of the Admiralty of the 'unsupportable losses' he had sustained 'by the manifest piracy of certain Dutch at Rotterdam'. Failing to get satisfaction from the authorities in the Netherlands, he 'prayed relief, there being no one who had suffered so much by the Dutch as he has'.

So many prizes were being taken into Bristol Channel ports, including Minehead, that a receiver was appointed who was able to claim five per cent. on all goods seized and sold. He complained that collecting the money had not been easy, and it was an expensive business because he was expected to prepare three or four copies of his accounts.[2]

Foreign pirate ships, not to be outdone, continued to retaliate, and when two barques of 50 tons each, bound out of Minehead with passengers for Ireland, were set upon and captured by a Turkish vessel, and soon afterwards a Bristol ship was also taken, the mayor and commonalty of Bristol besought the king to provide a man-of-war to defend the coast.

Charles, however, was more interested in collecting ship money than in providing men-of-war as convoys. He ordered Bristol, Bridgwater and all maritime places between Gloucester and Minehead to club together to 'set forth a ship of 800 tons for 26 weeks, manned with 260 men and fully equipped'.[3]

Increasingly the king's high-handed actions and his continued imposition of taxes without the sanction of parliament moved the country towards civil war. As soon as that war broke out, Charles sent the Lord Lieutenant of Somerset westwards with a commission of array, the royal authority for raising troops. The Lord Lieutenant, William Seymour, had recently been created Marquis of Hertford, and was now Lieutenant-General of the Western Counties, a commission which covered an area from Oxford to Land's End and from Southampton to Radnor and Cardigan. He took with him, Clarendon says, a number of gentlemen 'of the prime quality and interest in the western parts', including Sir Ralph Hopton. If he hoped to find it easy to raise support for the king in Somerset, he was disappointed; Parliamentary sympathies were strong in the county, as in others in the west. Driven out of Wells, he moved to Sherborne, only to find himself surrounded by opposing forces under the Earl of Bedford. Hertford held a 'court of war' which decided that a retreat was necessary, 'but whither, it was verie hard to say'. Eventually he accepted the advice of some Somerset gentlemen to march straight to Minehead (Clarendon's spelling is Mynneard) where he was assured that he would be able to commandeer one of the Welsh barques that called regularly every Thursday. With Bedford in pursuit, he arrived at Minehead and quartered some of his men there and some in Dunster, though his demand for the surrender of the castle was rejected by Thomas Luttrell, who had inherited on the death of his father in 1629. Thomas's wife Jane was the daughter of a keen Parliamentarian, Sir Francis Popham, and it is said that she personally ordered the defenders to fire on the Royalists.

Learning of Hertford's approach, Thomas Luttrell had added 100 men to his garrison and ordered the removal of the sails and rudders of ships in Minehead harbour. The Marquis, unable to escape by sea at once, is said to have shut himself up with his force in a strong inn, but it would have needed to be a very large inn to accommodate his four or five hundred followers and their horses. Two days after his arrival he managed to seize one or two Welsh coal boats which had not been deprived of their rudders and sails; in these he sailed for Wales with his foot soldiers and baggage, while Sir Ralph Hopton, with about fifty dragoons and 110 horses, rode down to Cornwall by way of Dulverton and Barnstaple.

Within a few months the Marquis of Hertford had gathered a large force in Wales and marched back into England, driving the Earl of Stamford out of Hereford. By February 1643, he was holding Cirencester. Sir Ralph Hopton, fresh from victories in Cornwall, rejoined him with Prince Maurice and a large body of Royalists. During June 1643, this army obtained the submission of Taunton and Bridgwater.

To Thomas Luttrell, the king's cause seemed to be on the verge of total victory. Royalists in ships commandeered in Wales were active in the Bristol Channel; they blockaded Minehead, preventing coal and other goods from entering the harbour. On one occasion a force under Captain Paulet landed and 'constrained the

27. Coming from Minehead early in the Civil War, the Royalist Marquis of Hertford would have seen the recently-completed Dunster Castle much as it appears here, apart from some differences in the towers. However, 18th-century drawings show that even as late as 1764, the outline of the Tor was distinct, as it had not yet been concealed by trees.

28. This photograph, showing the main entrance of Dunster Castle as it appeared after Salvin had completed his work, may be compared with F. F. Lyte's drawing of it made some sixty years earlier. The castle and its surrounding park were given to the National Trust in 1976 by Lt. Col. Walter Luttrell, M.C. Its magnificent 17th-century stables, with their ranges of great pillared stalls, lie on the slope below the castle. The National Trust's shop is housed in one part of the building.

inhabitants to yield to any taxation, and to submit themselves servants and slaves to every poore base companion, to save their throats from being cut'. Captain Paulet made an attempt on Dunster Castle, but the defenders opened fire and killed several of his men, or so it was reported, although Dunster burial registers record the death of only one soldier in 1643, and that was in March. However, Captain Paulet is said to have uttered vengeful threats as he withdrew.

All these happenings may have helped to shake Thomas Luttrell's nerve. Perhaps also he was ill; he died the following year. In any case he decided to surrender the castle rather than risk more bloodshed. His Royalist nephew, Colonel Wyndham, played a large part in persuading him, and took over as commander of the castle. Thomas was compelled to pay a fine of £1,000, in two parts, towards the expenses of Hertford's troops.

For more than a year Colonel Wyndham was secure at Dunsterbut, from the time of the Parliamentary victory at Marston Moor in July 1644, Royalist fortunes began to fade. The king sent Prince Charles, then a boy of 15, to Bristol in the spring of 1645, in the hope that he might raise new levies. Plague had broken out in the city, and the Prince moved to Dunster, not knowing that the little borough was equally full of infection. The death rate there for the whole of 1645 was about five times that of a normal year, and as there was no fighting, it may be that four soldiers recorded in the burial registers between 2 April and 28 May were victims of plague.

The Prince spent barely two weeks in the castle – the only place in Somerset still in Royalist hands – before being sent on to Barnstaple. Although Minehead's sympathies were Parliamentarian, they evidently felt bound to welcome the young Prince in the customary way; the churchwardens' accounts contain an entry 'Given the ringers in beere at several tymes when the Prince and other great men came into the towne, 14 shillings'. They also had to pay the Prince's footman 5s. 6d. 'which he claymed due to him for his fee'.

Although in 1641 some soldiers, perhaps troops passing to Ireland, had contributed 17s. 6d. to the poor box in St Michael's church, and 'Mr. Jephson and Troopers' had given more than a pound, an entry of a very different kind appears in 1645: 'Lost of the church Stocke beinge plundered when the Lord Goringe was here'. Goring was one of the most hated Royalist commanders, a drunken, violent and rapacious man. In July 1645 he was defeated at Langport. The next day he reached Dunster Castle, and wrote a report of the battle to Lord Digby, dating it 'Dunster, July 12, 1645, 1 at Morning, Saturday'. It must have been during this brief visit (the next day he marched on to Barnstaple) that his undisciplined men plundered the church.

The Parliamentarians could not for long leave Dunster Castle as an unmolested Royalist stronghold. Two thousand men were levied in Somerset for the New Model Army in October 1645, all the men of the Hundred of Williton and Freemanors being called on to enlist.[4] Reinforced with fresh troops, one of the ablest Parliamentarian commanders, Colonel Robert Blake – later to serve successfully against the Dutch as an admiral – was sent to call on Francis Wyndham to surrender. When Wyndham refused, a siege began which was to drag on until the following spring.

One of the Royalist publications of the time, 'Mercurius Academicus', put out a highly romantic story about Wyndham's mother being taken prisoner and defying

her captors when threatened with death if her son did not capitulate; it also claimed
that Sir Richard Grenville had marched from Cornwall and raised the siege. All of
this was apparently fiction. There were indeed two attempts to relieve the castle, the
second of which, in February 1646, managed to drive Blake away long enough to
supply the defenders with gunpowder and animals for slaughter. But in the months
that followed there were further Royalist reverses in the west. Although Blake's
attempts to mine the castle had little success, luckily for the building's survival, he
was reinforced to such a degree that it became clear to Wyndham that it was useless
to hold out any longer; he surrendered on honourable terms after a siege of about
160 days. Minehead rejoiced, and paid its ringers 4s. 8d. to celebrate.

After Francis Wyndham had marched away to join the king – in the chivalrous
fashion of the time he was allowed to go forth freely with his men, drums beating and
colours flying – George Luttrell, who had been living at his family's house at
Marshwood, presumably prepared to occupy the castle once again; his father had
died in 1644 and he was now lord of Dunster. He had just come of age.

It was at this point that his Minehead tenants perhaps decided that they would
begin with the new master as they meant to go on. They presented him with a
statement affirming that all the ancient customs used in the manor, but never
previously written down – or so they claimed – 'are to be observed and kept and not
to be infringed by the lord of the said Mannor nor by his heirs or assignes'. It
contained 32 items. Referring to themselves as Customary Suitors, the tenants
asserted, among other things, that they had the right to keep their 'sheepe and other
Cattell' on the lord's commons and wastes, i.e. Minehead Hill, Periton Hill, North
Hill and Minehead Marsh; to 'take and break' in the lord's commons and wastes,
paying 12 pence an acre at Michaelmas; and to fell oak, ash and elms growing on
their tenements 'at their will and pleasure without denial'.

At the same time they acknowledged duties, such as 'viewing the Lordes Boundes
at the command of the Lordes Steward', grinding their corn at the lord's mill and
keeping the water-course running to the lord's warren. In addition they were
prepared to clean the mill pond yearly on the Thursday of Whitsun week, expecting
to be rewarded with a dinner by the miller, and to attend the lord's court on law days,
again receiving a dinner afterwards. Moreover they were still prepared to accept that,
when a customary tenant died, the 'best living beast' should be given up as a heriot,
but required that a widow should keep her dead husband's tenement as long as she
did not remarry. Most remarkably of all, perhaps, they had no objection to the
ancient feudal requirement that no tenant should 'carry his work out of the said
Mannor but to be employed in the said Mannor'. Most of the remaining items deal
with the copyhold system under which they held their tenements.[5]

In the aftermath of the war, parliament exacted fines for 'delinquency' from the
more influential people who had favoured the king's cause. A William Sandford who
had 'adhered to the forces against Parliament' was fined £134, though a John Norris,
who had raised a troop of horse for the king, and whose son John had been at Oxford
when the city surrendered, got off more lightly, having to pay £22. Some people were
dunned by both sides; a Lewish Lashbrooke, for instance, of Minehead, had been
compelled to pay £40 to the Royalists when they imprisoned him, and then a further
£50 to Colonel Blake towards the siege of Dunster Castle. Others changed sides, like

John Question, born in Minehead, who had practised as a surgeon in Dunster. Originally he accepted a Royalist commission, but later deserted, perhaps because he was a man of property, and houses which he owned in Dunster were burned by the king's forces. He put his medical skills at the service of the Parliamentarians and contributed £40 to the expenses of Blake's siege.

Maintaining the post-war forces was an expensive business. A Charles Steynings wrote in February 1648 to his 'worthy ffriende and loving uncle', John Willoughby, that £15 a week was being charged against 'our little hundred' (i.e. the Hundred of Carhampton) towards the quartering of 100 soldiers of Colonel Popham and his company 'relating to the Castle of Dunster', and shortly before that they had had 40 dragoons of Sir Hardress Waller's brigade for a month.[6]

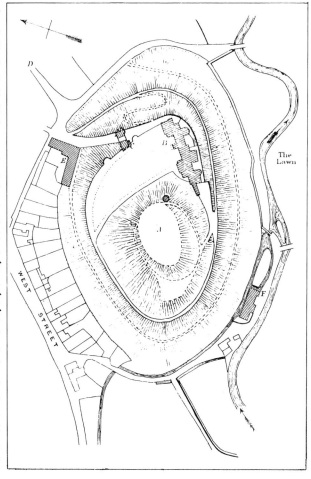

In 1650 one of the strangest men ever to spend time in Dunster Castle arrived there, not as a member of the occupying force but as a prisoner. He was the tireless pamphleteer, William Prynne. As it happened he was a Somerset man, born in 1600 at Swainswick and educated at Bath Grammar School before going up to Oxford. Throughout his life he showed remarkable powers of disapproval of selected people, institutions or opinions. Beginning with an appeal to parliament, in 1627, to suppress anything written against Calvinist doctrine, and with attacks on the fashions and follies of his age, he moved on to a condemnation, at great length, of stage plays, *Histrio-Matrix*. Parts of this, interpreted as implied criticism of both Charles I and his queen, earned him a Star Chamber trial, imprisonment and harsh penalties, including the loss of his ears and a spell in the pillory. In prison he wrote diatribes against the episcopacy, and was again pilloried and branded with the letters SL for seditious libeller. When he was released by the Long Parliament, he continued his non-stop pamphleteering, now in the Parliamentary cause. A qualified

29. This plan of Dunster Castle, made at the same time as F. F. Lyte's drawing of the north-west front, shows: A. the Tor and Keep; B. Lower Ward and House; C. Ancient Entrance and Lower Gatehouse; D. Approach from the town; E. Stables; F. Mill (Lyte).

lawyer, he conducted the case against Archbishop Laud with savage vindictiveness. He became an M.P. after the Civil War; his next targets for criticism were, first, the Army, and then the taxes levied by the Commonwealth. It was this last piece of outspokenness that brought him what he called his 'illegal close imprisonment' in Dunster Castle.

Described as one who 'gloated in leafy folios ... one of the greatest paper-worms which ever crept into old books and musty records', Prynne found the Dunster Castle muniments of the greatest interest (after the Restoration, Charles II was to appoint him Keeper of the Records in the Tower) and, with the approval of young George Luttrell, whiled away the eight months of his stay in the castle sorting out the 'confused chaos' of the family papers and cataloguing them, a task which earned him the gratitude of later historians.

*Chapter Seven*

# Of Sheep and Ships:
## The Trade of Dunster and Minehead

For centuries, Dunster earned its living from the wool trade. Leland, in the 1540s, stated flatly 'The towne of Dunstorre maketh clothe'.

Cloth making began there as early as the 13th century. A manorial survey dated 1266 shows that among the tenants were a dyer and three weavers, two of the latter being women. At various dates between 1259 and 1376 a rental of 13s. 4d. a year was paid for a tucking or fulling mill, and by 1418 there were no fewer than four fulling mills. Towards the end of the 15th century, dyers were evidently busy: three of them were fined for polluting the Avill as it ran between Dunster and the Haven with woad water. As a result an ordinance decreed that no one was to throw 'le wodewater' into the lord's stream before eight o'clock at night, on pain of 40 pence for each offence, a stiff fine at the time.

The town gave its name to a type of cloth: an Act of James I's reign, in 1607, lays down that 'every broadcloth commonly called ... Dunsters, made in the western part of Somerset-shire ... shall contain, being thoroughly wet, between 12 and 13 yards'. When treated and dried, they were to weigh at least thirty pounds per cloth.

In 1609 George Luttrell built the octagonal yarn market which still stands, a pleasing little structure pictorially represented countless times. In the Civil War it was damaged, and another George Luttrell, grandson of the first, had it repaired; his initials and the date 1647 are pierced into the vane that surmounts it.

In the early 19th century a tradition lingered that 24 master clothiers from the town had formerly been in the habit of attending fairs at Bristol and Exeter and that its market, held on Fridays, had been 'the most considerable one in the western part of the county'. The spinning of yarn by hand was done by women on farms 'from the mistress to the apprentice maid, and the wives and daughters of the labourers' in the intervals of their ordinary work. The yarn was sold to clothiers who came to Dunster market from many other towns in the district.[1]

In the 1790s the Avill was still driving two fulling mills, as well as one oil mill and no fewer than six grist mills.[2] However, 'the large manufacture of kersey cloths' that had existed at the beginning of the 18th century had now almost wholly moved to other places. By 1830 the only fulling mills remaining were described as decaying; a factory at Frackford was in ruins, and terraces on the southern slopes of Grabhurst (Grabbist), where in the first half of the 18th century a Dunster clother called William Leigh had the right to set up racks for drying cloth, were no longer used.[3]

The 1831 census shows that Dunster had a population of 895 (today it has 793) living in 179 houses. There were 183 families; 84 worked in agriculture, 78 in trade, manufacturing or handicraft, while 21 were not included in either category. There were coopers, saddlers, painters and glaziers, five boot and shoe makers, three blacksmiths, a wheelwright, and agents for the Atlas and Norwich Union fire

30. Dunster with the Yarn Market, by J. C. Buckler (1821). Savage, writing in 1830, mentions just four streets in Dunster: Church Street, West Street, Water or Gallox Street, and Fore Street, now High Street. This engraving shows, beyond the Yarn Market, the 'long range of ruinous shambles and timber-built market hall', which were soon to be demolished by John Fownes Luttrell. The *Luttrell Arms* can be seen here in the left foreground.

31. Dunster High Street (once Chepynge Street, later Fore Street), a century later than Buckler's engraving, yet hardly less peaceful – ironically, while war raged elsewhere. Henry Fownes Luttrell's Conygar Tower stands out on its hill.

insurance companies. Apart from ten general shopkeepers there was a nurseryman, an earthenware dealer, a clothes dealer and a wine and spirit merchant. The Luttrells had set up a charity school and there were two private day schools and a boarding school.

The *Luttrell Arms* was the most important inn. It is thought to have been a house used by the Abbots of Cleeve, near Washford; upstairs is the Abbot's Room, full of fine carving. George Luttrell carried out alterations in the 1620s, when William Arnold was building his castle-house; a plaster-work overmantel in an upper room is similar to one in the castle.

Other Dunster inns of the period were the *Coach and Horses* (like the *Luttrell Arms*, a posting house), the *Bristol Arms*, the *Castle*, the *Red Lion*, the *Stag's Head* and the *Horse and Crooks*, this last name indicating that it was a packhorseman's inn.

Minehead, too, had its clothiers. From medieval times it was a port at which Irish and Welsh wool was landed. A few years after an Act was passed prohibiting the export of wool from 'His Majesty's Isles' in 1615, another Act made certain exceptions: wool from Pembroke, Carmarthen, etc. might be transported to Minehead, as well as Bristol and Barnstaple, provided it was not then surreptitiously re-exported.

Around the middle of the 17th century a colony of Irish refugees, fleeing from Cromwell's harsh measures, established themselves in Minehead and acquired skills which they later took back to Ireland; it is thought to have been this group which helped to set up cloth-making in Dublin, Cork, Clonmel and Kinsale. Competition

32. A view of Grabbist, formerly Grabhurst (in old deeds Grobefast) Hill, looking across the lower valley of the river Avill. Although the Avill is today no more than a meandering stream, in the Middle Ages it drove grist and fulling mills and its mouth was a harbour from which ships sailed to France and Spain.

from Ireland contributed to the decline of the industry in Somerset towns, including Minehead.[4] The importation of wool from Ireland dropped from a peak of nearly 65,000 stone in 1722 to under 7,000 stone in 1740, and apparently ceased altogether in the 1760s.

Nevertheless it seems that some manufacture of serge and other coarse cloth went on in Minehead until the end of the 18th century. In the burial register, few men are shown as having a connection with the industry, but this may be because, here as elsewhere, it remained largely a cottage industry carried on by women and children. Defoe remarked that there were 11,000 looms at work in Taunton when he went there in 1724. Significantly and, to modern minds, horrifyingly, he added that 'there was not a child in the town, or in the villages round it, of five years old but, if it was not neglected [sic] by its parents, could earn its own bread'. Even if similar child labour existed in Minehead, and even if the unfortunate children died, their occupation would not be recorded in the burial register; those of women were ignored.

The entrepreneurs who employed the home weavers could prosper. In 1749 a Minehead clothier, John Devonshire, was doing well enough to take out a policy with the Sun Insurance Company, insuring his business for £400; in 1766 a clothier and dyer, Andrew Blake, with his dye house in Bampton Street, insured his business with the Sun for £900.[5]

33. A view of Dunster Castle in 1853, showing the mill and the two neighbouring bridges over the Avill (Rock).

However, it was shipping, rather than sheep, that sustained the town, despite many difficulties over maintaining the harbour. Its least profitable use was perhaps as an embarkation port for troops being sent to Ireland. When the Royalist Marquis of Ormonde was besieging Dublin in 1646, shipping was demanded to carry a Parliamentarian regiment of foot at the most reasonable rates that could be agreed. Soldiers' pay was 14 pence a week, with fourpence deducted to pay quarters. Men were to receive a month's pay before embarking, and every man was to have five shillings' worth of victuals shipped with him for the voyage; seasickness, it seems, was not anticipated.[6] Three years later, when Cromwell defeated Ormonde with great brutality, ringers of St Michael's church, Minehead, rang the bells in celebration, but there was sorrow in the town as well: the churchwardens paid the expenses of two men to travel to Taunton to petition on behalf of the parish 'to procure reliefe of the adjacent parishes for the poore Widdows and fatherless Children whose husbands were cast away in transportation of soldiers for the service of Ireland'.

During the Interregnum, Minehead's commerce evidently continued busily. Port dues recorded during the first quarter of 1648 show vessels bringing goods from Watchet, Bristol, north and south Devon and Youghal. Others arrived from as far away as Amsterdam, St Kitts and New England. Cargoes included cows, horses, pigs, wool, corn, wine and tobacco.[7]

The old problem of piratical attack in the Bristol Channel was as acute as it had been before the Civil War began. In 1655 Minehead joined with Barnstaple, Bideford and Ilfracombe to seek help from the Commissioners of the Navy. Pointing out that they had always received all sorts of commodities, such as those listed above, they complained that Spanish men-of-war were infesting the coasts to such an extent that they could not trade safely; they besought their honours to afford 'a couple of small nimble frigottes to waft our Vesselles foorth and back'. There were 15 signatures on behalf of Minehead, one of them, almost inevitably, being Robert Quirke.[8]

Frigates were duly provided. There was the *Fox*, escorting ships sailing from Cork and Youghal in 1658 with corn for Bristol and Minehead, or convoying a dozen barks to Ireland; there was the *Harp*, convoying 40 sail from Ireland, laden with wool, cattle and sheep 'some for Barnstaple, 14 or 15 for Minehead'. On one occasion a large convoy of 30 or 40 ships, 'the Irish fleet bound for Minehead', caused alarm by being mistaken for a French fleet.

Early in Charles II's reign Minehead people were wondering at the delay of the Virginia fleet in Irish ports: 'some say that southerly winds detain them, some that they want a convoy, some that the seamen are afraid to come home lest they be pressed'.[9] (At that period, press masters were busy along the coast; they considered that Minehead, Watchet and Porlock could provide 50 men if armed force was used. In these circumstances, it was understandable that some men were chary of coming home.)

Large groups of vessels passing up and down the Bristol Channel became an accustomed sight, and must have been one of considerable beauty. In July 1667, for instance, while the Virginia fleet of 27 sail passed up-channel, bound for Bristol, thirty or more ships, escorted by six or seven men-of-war, were sighted heading westwards, bound for the English Channel. The guard ships were effective; when the *Garland* was escorting 40 ships from Plymouth heading for Bristol and Wales, they met two French sloops and a Dutch vessel known as a caper, which bore away as soon as they saw the *Garland*. At this time England was at war with Holland; there was a rumour that Dutch ships were in Milford Haven, and beacons were lit on the Welsh coast. Lundy was reported to be 'very slenderly guarded ... if the Dutch should take the island it would block up the Severn'.[10]

At the beginning of his reign, Charles II passed an Act forbidding the importation of cattle from Ireland as a 'common and public nuisance'; any cattle brought in were to be seized and forfeited, with the ship that carried them. Nevertheless, the following year a Minehead correspondent, writing to James Hickes, Clerk to the Post Office, reported that a dozen small barks had left for Ireland to fetch more cattle and sheep; he supposed they intended to continue carrying cattle as formerly until parliament met. He considered the Act a foolish one, remarking that 'the King will lose £3,000 or £4,000 in the customs'. At intervals he reported the arrival of more cattle and, in August 1667, 'the town is glad that the parliament is put by, as they are afraid of being questioned for importing Irish cattle'.

Although he noted two months later that 'The late proclamation has put an absolute stop to the irregular trade of importing Irish cattle, so that there is no fear of being troubled any more with those kind creatures', about two years later a shipment of cattle was brought into Minehead harbour, whereupon both the animals and the vessel that carried them were held and sold. In accordance with the provisions of the Act, part of the money obtained from the sale was invested by the churchwardens and overseers of Minehead parish. They bought a 20-acre farm in Ottery St Mary, Devon, with the idea that rent from the property should be used for the benefit of the poor of the town, and this came to be known as the Cow Charity.

Over the years some of the trustees of the charity, including a certain William Warren and one of the Luttrell family, managed to get into their own hands a total

34. The origin of this building is not known. It may be of the 15th century. In the 19th and at the beginning of the 20th centuries it was in use as the office in which the business of the Luttrell estates was carried on. Later uses have included a furniture store and a tea room. Today its frontage is partly obscured by stalls selling fruit, vegetables and plants. A guide book of some seventy years ago suggested that it might become a museum of West Somerset Antiquities, but regrettably this was not taken up (Hancock).

of about £1,100, while the poor, presumably, received nothing. In 1821 the churchwardens and overseers presented a petition to the Lord Chancellor, as a result of which an enquiry was held and Warren and Luttrell were ordered to disgorge the money they had accumulated. Remarkably, when new trustees were appointed, the two erring gentlemen were among them. However, the £1,100 was invested in 3 per cent. consols, and from then on a certain amount of interest was received by the poor in the form of coats and blankets or small sums of money. In the late 19th and early 20th centuries the charity's investments were producing £70 a year, spent on clothing and blankets for needy cases; by 1914 the same sum was being distributed in grants to Minehead Hospital 'for the provision of nurses and in relieving cases of necessity in money and in kind'. Twenty years later this arrangement, and the sum available, had not changed, according to Kelly's *Directory for Somerset* for 1936.

During the second half of the 17th century, the increase in customs duties made smuggling a paying game, and it flourished accordingly. In 1682 Charles II sent his surveyor-general of customs, William Culliford, to Somerset. In Minehead, Culliford took evidence from a number of informants, who told him of hogsheads of wine and of tobacco, casks of brandy and packets of Irish linen and frieze being landed by night and carried to houses on the quay, from which they were later transported, also by night, in wagons to Taunton. Local tidesmen and the riding surveyor, whose business it should have been to track down the smugglers, had evidently been turning a blind eye. In fact one of the tidesmen, who was also a bailiff and kept an alehouse, did confess to 'several frauds and miscarryages in the said Port', but before Culliford was able to question him fully he was prevailed on to deny his confession 'upon assurance from Colonel Luttrell (as I have been informed) that he shall still be continued in his employment'. What was more, it was reported that Colonel Luttrell, who was a J.P., had one informant whipped, on the complaint that he was 'a night walker, and that they, meaning the merchants, could not doe their business for this Informer and such Rogues'. Finding that no one in the town would undertake the whipping, Luttrell sent one of his own servants from Dunster Castle to give the unfortunate man a hundred stripes: a neat example of squire supporting smugglers and punishing their opponents.

35. This doorway may still be seen on the west side of the Manor Office building, in Summerland Street (Harper).

Minehead was, of course, by no means the only place on the Somerset coast where smugglers were active. In neighbouring Watchet, for example, Culliford reported that within the past 10 years 'the whole town has grown exceeding rich', and his final verdict was that no custom house in the county passed the test of enquiry.

Francis Luttrell, a colonel in the Somerset Militia, played some part in the fighting at the time of Monmouth's rebellion in 1685, although accounts differ as to whether his support was for King James or Monmouth. In view of his position, it would be reasonable to suppose the former, and this seems to be confirmed by a report that, after the king had ordered the raising of the Militia in Somerset on 13 June 1685, 'Colonel Luttrell, with those already in arms, entered Taunton that day and marched out in the afternoon'. It seems that their destination was Chard; in that town Luttrell is said to have commented that the rebel soldiers 'knew not their captains' and had no order among them.[11]

On 8 July the bells of Minehead parish church rang to celebrate the defeat of the rebels at the battle of Sedgemoor – but they rang much louder and longer, judging by the amount paid to the ringers, when William of Orange was proclaimed King in 1688.[12] Like many people in the west country, Colonel Luttrell welcomed the new king, and joined him at Exeter. At William's request he raised an infantry regiment which was eventually to become the Green Howards.

Short-lived like so many of those who, over the centuries, owned Dunster and Minehead, he died in 1690 at the age of only 31, leaving large debts, despite the fact that he had married a rich Dorsetshire heiress, Mary Tregonwell. After her husband's death, Mary Luttrell may have bought at least some of the contents of Dunster Castle to prevent their going to creditors. The diary of Narcissus Luttrell, kinsman of Colonel Luttrell, records on 19 November 1696, 'Yesterday morning a sudden fire hapned in Mrs. Luttrell's house in St James Street, being newly and richly furnished, which burnt it to the ground, the lady herself narrowly escaping, and 'tis said she lost in plate, jewels etc. to the value of £10,000'.[13]

Within a few weeks Mary Luttrell had married again. Gossip claimed that her new husband had bet a large sum – though one wonders whether this was before the fire – that he would marry the rich widow. He was Jacob Bancks, a Swede born in Stockholm in 1633. Having come to England as secretary to his uncle, the Swedish Ambassador, he was commissioned in the British Navy in 1690. 'He commanded several ships from 1691 to 1696, was a brave naval officer, and was at the siege of Cork, and the action at Malaga, in which last he lost his ship', Savage says. After his marriage to Mary Luttrell he retired on half-pay, and was knighted in 1699. From 1698 until 1714 he was M.P. for Minehead, and in 1719 he presented the town with a statue of Queen Anne in white alabaster, the work of Francis Bird.

The statue was set up on a pedestal in the parish church; the men who carried it there were given 2s. 6d. for beer. It was protected by iron railings, which can be seen in old photographs of the interior of the church. From time to time it became necessary to clean it. In 1723, for instance, the job cost 1s. 6d., but by 1742 either the statue had become much dirtier, or wages had increased dramatically: the charge then was 22 shillings. When the church was restored in 1887 the statue was removed. Page, writing in about 1889, said that it was then in the hands of a builder, awaiting removal to the new Town Hall, but an official guide to Minehead published in about 1920 says that it lay for some time derelict after being taken from the church. Finally, in 1893, it was moved to the place it still occupies, protected from the weather by a marble canopy paid for by the parishioners. On the sandstone supporting pillars significant dates in the queen's reign are inscribed, from the capture of Gibraltar and

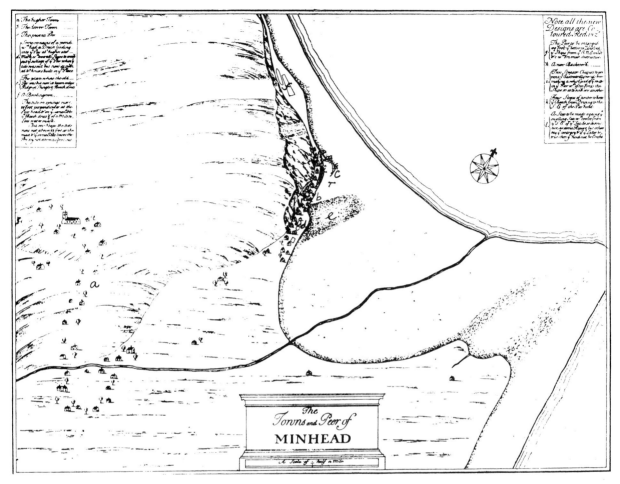

36. A plan of Minehead *c.*1704. The text in the top left-hand corner reads:

a. The higher Town
b. The lower Town
c. The present Pier
d. Some remains of a pond which had a Drain leading into ye Pier about highwater mark with severall sluices to wash out ye sullage of ye Pier when ye tide was out but now it's ruined and houses built in ye Place
e. The Place where the old Pier was but now it's becom only a Ridge of Shingle and Beach stones
f. A Bowling Green
 The tide on springs rises 28 foot perpendicular at the Pier head and on ye same Ebbs ye Beach dries three-quarters of a mile to low water mark. But on Neaps the tide rises not above 22 foot at the most and ye same Ebbs leave the Pier dry not above 20 foot out.

The Text in the top right-hand corner reads:
g. Ye Pier to be enlarged 100 foot ye better to Landlock ye Ships from ye N.E. winds, etc., which are most destructive
h. A new backwork
i. Two Stops or Cheques to prevent ye Eastwardly winds from making a whirlpool of ye Water in ye Pier which often forces ye Ships to sink one another
k. Four stops of timber to keep ye Beach from Driving to the S.E. of the Pier Head
l. A Stop to be made against ye swelling Sea which comes from ye S.E.; if ye Sea be so destructive as Some Report but others say to the contrary and if ye Latter be true then ye head be not erected.

The letters g to l are not marked on the plan, presumably because the items they indicate are part of the projected new harbour works and do not yet exist (Hancock).

the battle of Blenheim in 1704 to other battles of the war of the Spanish Succession, the Union with Scotland in 1707 and the Treaty of Utrecht of 1713.

The son of Colonel Francis and Mary Luttrell, baptised with his mother's maiden name, Tregonwell, was a boy of seven when his father died. He did not live to attain his majority; on his death in 1703 the Luttrell estates went to his uncle, George Alexander Luttrell. Shortly before this an Act was obtained in Tregonwell's name for 'recovering, securing and keeping in repair the harbour of Minehead, for the benefit and support of the navigation of this kingdom'. Some of the wording of the preamble is identical with that of a similar Act obtained for Ilfracombe in 1727; it said that Minehead's harbour 'had by long experience been found to be of great benefit to the western parts of this kingdom, and to all seafaring men, who, by any stress of weather, are driven upon that coast'.

Tregonwell's father, the young colonel, 'at his command and cost', had caused large-scale repairs to be carried out, and huge stones set in place as a protection against the sea. A brass plate was affixed to the pier recording that the work was done in 1682, but presumably the fact that that was the year of William Culliford's visit to inspect the custom house had no bearing on the matter.

Yet now, just 20 years later, the pier was said to be 'so choked and barred by the Beach which had been thrown into it by the violence of the Sea and alterations of the Tides, that unless some speedy and effectual Care were taken to stop the growing Beach ... by building out a new Head, and other Works, and daily clearing and repairing the same, the said Harbour would become useless to the Kingdom, prejudicial to Trade, and dangerous to Navigation, to the impoverishing of the Inhabitants of Minehead'.

The Act of 1701-2 granted the Luttrells the right to charge increased duties on all goods imported or exported to or from Minehead for a period of 21 years, and at intervals during the next two centuries, later sovereigns extended these powers. The charge on wool was a halfpenny for every stone, which were still 18-pound stones. Other duties were twopence a ton on salt, twopence a quarter on corn, twopence a chaldron on coal, and sixpence a ton on various other goods. These were 'over and besides the ancient and customary duties and acknowledgements already accustomed to be paid to the said Tregonwell Luttrell and his ancestors'. British ships taking shelter had to pay one or two shillings according to size; those from Ireland, France, Spain and other parts of Europe, or trading with the American colonies, paid more. Any coming from Asia or Africa were required to pay ten shillings.[14]

Licensed privateering by Somerset vessels was still going on at this time; in 1702 a ship of 100 tons sailed out of Minehead under letters of marque granted to her captain, William Rogers. She was owned by his brothers, Edward and James Rogers, merchants, and was accordingly named *The Three Brothers*. She carried 30 men and eight guns, as well as six barrels of powder, 30 rounds of great shot and about ten hundredweight of small shot. Small arms included cutlasses, muskets, pistols and blunderbusses. Victualled for nine months and provided with two suits of sails and ample spare cordage, she was well prepared for a roving commission.[15] Another vessel, the *Queen Anne* galley, also the property of Minehead merchants, sailed on similar voyages.

The harbour from which these ships set out was still, it seems, in a poor state. When Colonel Alexander Luttrell inherited on the death of his nephew Tregonwell, he did not at once make any move to improve it. The new charges must have been very unpopular; perhaps he waited for monies to accumulate. Eventually he commissioned a cheap substitute for the sort of structure that was needed: a wooden quay head, using local timber. Within six or seven years 'the Sea-worms had gotten into it, whereby the Timber on the back-side of the Key was very much perished and decayed'.

It was no longer the concern of Alexander Luttrell; he outlived Tregonwell by only eight years. His son, another Alexander, was an infant; his widow and trustees appointed under the Act of Parliament of 10 years earlier applied for an extension of the rights granted, and this was agreed on condition that a large lantern was fixed at the quay head and lit nightly from 1 September to 31 March as a guide to shipping.

Mrs. Luttrell and the trustees commissioned the building of a substantial stone wall, 12 feet wide at the base, narrowing to six feet at the top, round the outside of the new quay or pier 'from the Sun Dial situate on the Old Key to the South end corner of the New Key'. The Watchet mason to whom the work was given was also to build, by Michaelmas 1714, another stone wall 'from the South end or corner of the New Key home to the Old Key inside of the Harbour ... allowing to every rope of Wall of 20 feet long two Hogsheads of good lime'.

Unfortunately, around Christmas 1715, a tremendous storm shattered the new walls all round the old quay 'and broke down and damnified some of the wharfe walls and Houses', so that the mason had to start repairs without delay. He also contracted, in June 1716, to build a long high wall on the wharf and raise the old quay wall by six feet.

Mrs. Luttrell was now incensed to find that some merchants from Tiverton, Taunton and Minehead itself were petitioning parliament to make Watchet a staple port to draw off Minehead's trade. They resented having to weigh their goods at Minehead's Town Hall and pay a fee for doing so. Mrs. Luttrell, or her legal advisers, drew up a detailed document, setting out the history of the pier from the reign of Henry VII, when Sir Hugh had built his small quay, and giving an account of all expenses incurred by the Luttrell family over the centuries since that time. It put the blame for 'the strife and discord that there now is in the Borough and in opposing the Family of Dunster Castle' on Quakers and dissenters.[16]

It also referred to a disputed election of 1713, when two candidates opposed those approved by the Luttrells, and brought charges of bribery against them. However, counter-charges were laid by the Luttrells, and the election was declared void. 'So the Whig party was put to great charges and at last very much was disappointed ... But if they had ... had success therein, then they had a design to get their former charter and ... had their petitions in readiness to be delivered to the King, and boasted very much about it'.

This document bears the date '22 August 1716' at the end of the final set of accounts. It seems that the people did in fact petition for a renewal of their charter a few months later: the appeal of 'the gentlemen, merchants, traders and principal inhabitants' was put before the Privy Council – chaired by the Prince of Wales, 'Guardian of ye Kingdom' – on 17 December 1716. It admitted that the port and harbour had been kept in good repair since Alexander Luttrell obtained the right to charge special duties, and that trade had flourished in recent years. But the borough was now so populous, it went on, that 'without power and Rule of Government within itself (of which it is wholly destitute) the said Borough will be subject to great disorders and its trade (by which Considerable Revenue accrewes to your Majesty) in danger of being once more lost'. It lacked the power 'to compell Strangers resorting thither to pay their debts incurred during their Abode there before their departure thence, such strangers frequently going off by sea'.

The petitioners therefore humbly prayed his Majesty to restore and confirm their earlier charter; they suggested the appointment of a Portreeve and Coroner, a Recorder and Senior Capital Burgess, 12 Capital Burgesses, a Steward and a Sergeant-at-Mace, bailiff and keeper of the gaol.[17]

It was no use: the Luttrell influence was still too strong, and no charter was granted. For that matter, Watchet did not become a staple port. Possibly the Quakers were penalised. A group of them had lived in the town since the 17th century, not long after the Society of Friends was formed. Their meeting house had stood at a corner of the street called the Butts, and they had rented their own burial ground 'walled and enclosed all round with good trees growing therein'; 12 Quakers were buried there between 1701 and 1704. However, according to a survey of Minehead which Hancock dates as *c.* 1740, but which may have been carried out a few years earlier, a newly-built Quakers' Meeting House in the Market Place, as well as the burying place, was in the lord's hands; this suggests that the Quakers had been forced to give up properties they rented, and many may have left the town.

The improvements to the quay must have been satisfactory, judging by an eye-witness report written some years after the Watchet mason had finished his work. Defoe set out on his tour of Britain in April 1722, and, heading west from London, probably reached Minehead before the end of the year. He found it a well-built town, full of rich merchants who traded chiefly with Ireland, but also with Virginia and the West Indies, resembling those of Barnstaple and Bristol in those respects. It had 'the best port, the safest harbour, in all those counties, at least, on this side. No ship is so big, but that it may come in, and no weather so bad, but the ships are safe when they are in'. He then adds something that makes the reader wonder what all the complaints, at the beginning of the century, about the harbour being useless to the kingdom, prejudicial to trade and dangerous to navigation had been about. For 'they told me, that in the great storm anno 1703, when in all the harbours and rivers in the county, the ships were blown on shore, wreck'd and lost, they suffered little or no damage in this harbour'.

*Chapter Eight*

# Overseeing the Poor

Minehead's churchwardens' accounts survive from the decade before the Civil War, while those of Dunster begin in the years of the Commonwealth.[1] Like similar accounts elsewhere, they provide much information, not only about church affairs, but concerning the way parishioners lived.

For Minehead church, a new organ was built by a Mr. Serridge in 1630 at a cost of £90, the pipes of the old one being sold off. A Mr. Rendell was asked to approve the new instrument; his charge for doing so was £5. The organist, Richard Jenkins, was paid £10 a year, but over the next hundred years organists' salaries dropped considerably; it was 1717 before anyone was again paid as much as £10. In 1671 a Henry Cozens was receiving only £3 a year as organist. He was evidently a craftsman with other skills; he was commissioned to brighten up the organ with colours, buying vermilion, saffron, blue, 'biss' (bice?) mastnet (mastic?) and glue for the job. This particular organ had a life of only some seventy years, being replaced by an instrument made by the German-born Thomas Schwarbrook, who charged nearly £120, and was given a treat at the *Plume of Feathers* when his work was finished.

From time to time one or other of St Michael's bells was re-hung or re-cast; when the Great Bell was re-hung in 1642, seamen from the harbour brought up 'blockes, roapes and similer' for the task, and the bell loft was repaired with timber brought from Dunster. Nearly a century later, when a bell needed to be re-cast, it was taken to and from Bristol by sea; the charge for the return voyage was 16s. 6d. As in most places in Britain, the bells were rung to celebrate important national events – coronations, royal weddings and births, battles in the Civil War, victories over Holland and Spain in the 1650s. When Charles II was proclaimed king the bells were rung and the royal arms repainted and restored to the church; during the Interregnum the old royal arms, which had been freshly painted in 1630 at the time Mr. Serridge installed the organ, had been whitewashed out. On each 5 November, the bells rang for 'the horred powder plote'. But by 1732 the cost of ringing had risen so much that the Vestry decided that in future only a monarch's birthday or coronation, the birthday of a Prince of Wales, and 5 November were to be celebrated by the bells. In 1765 there was a further economy; ringers might be paid for ringing on 5 November and 29 May (Oakapple Day) 'and on no other day at the expense of the parish'.

Two years before the Civil War began, the church rate stood at just over £45, but by 1646 it had dropped to a third of that figure, and in the 1650s a warrant was obtained to distrain those who refused to pay the rate. For a considerable time Minehead was without a vicar. Robert Knolles had been presented to the living in 1635 by the widow of Nicholas Prowse, the previous incumbent, who had bought the advowson in 1609. But Knolles was a fervent Royalist, with sons serving in the king's army; in 1643 his parishioners, largely Parliamentarian in sympathy, drove him out. It was not until the Restoration that another Nicholas Prowse, grandson of the first, reclaimed the advowson and appointed himself to the living.

Over the next 50 years it seems that the best way to become vicar of Minehead was to marry a widow. When Prowse died he left his household goods, valued at £64, to his widow, Anne, as well as the right of one presentation to the benefice 'for her future maintenance' and that of their five children. Anne Prowse quickly remarried and presented her new husband, Samuel Rooke. After Mr. Rooke's death there were two incumbents in six years, but in 1693 a young cleric named Robert Stone made an offer of £140 for the perpetual advowson which was accepted, it being remarked that 'the place was difficult to serve, and the profits consist much in casualties'. Robert Stone died in 1720, whereupon his widow presented Tristram Chave to the benefice, married him and, when he died not long afterwards, repeated both procedures with William Mogridge, who was probably a good deal younger than she was; he outlived her by many years. He lived to be 81, having been vicar of Minehead for 54 years and rector of Porlock for twenty-seven.

The advowson was bought by Mrs. Dorothy Luttrell, the widow of Colonel Alexander, in 1717 for £250 and 'two broad pieces of gold'; the deed of sale recorded that there was a very good vicarage house consisting of 'several good under rooms and chambers over them with courts and courtilages'. From then on the Luttrell family remained patrons of the living. Three of the four vicars of Minehead between 1780 and 1899 were Luttrells; the last of these, Alexander, served the parish for 67 years, dying at the age of 92 'having preserved his extraordinary vigour almost to the last'.

A number of early entries in the churchwardens' accounts concern the renting of seats in the church. In 1637 it was decided to charge parishioners five shillings to reserve a seat for life, but four years later demand seems to have led to a sharp increase in price; one pound was charged for a change of seat, and two pounds for the right to occupy a vacated seat. However, cheaper seats, presumably at the back of the church, could still be had for four shillings. In 1716, pews began to be numbered as though they were seats in a modern theatre. By this time any seat becoming vacant was at once let to the highest bidder. A new development was the building of pews by individuals for the use of themselves, their relations and friends. These were the old high pews; when Minehead church was restored in the 1880s by Piers St Aubyn, described as 'the most reckless of all the drastic restorers', they were all ripped out.

At Dunster the parish church had fixed pew rents, considerably lower than those at Minehead and some other west country parishes; the charge was only sixpence or a shilling a year, according to position. At the same time it was laid down that the sexton was to put two forms or benches in the middle aisle, 'one for the Poor Men, and the other for the Poor Women, to sit thereon during Divine Service'.

From the beginning of the Interregnum, when it was necessary to carry a pass to move about the country, churchwardens at Minehead had been handing out money to travellers in need. One man arrived bound for Ireland with a pass signed by Cromwell himself; the churchwardens cautiously gave him two shillings. Ship-wrecked sailors, old or poor ministers who 'came out of Ireland in great distress', poor women with children, refugees from the Great Fire of London (a collection was made in the town on behalf of the people of London) and from the sacking of Teignmouth by the French, all received help. But by 1691 the parish decided that 'disbursements upon travylling persons' had been excessive; in future there was to be a limit of threepence for a man, twopence for a woman and one penny for a child. Even this came to an end in the mid-18th century, when it was resolved not to give any money to travellers on any account whatsoever.

This was evidently a period for general economies. It had been customary in Minehead, as in many parishes, for the churchwardens to pay for the killing of 'vermints' – foxes, badgers, wild cats, hedgehogs, fitchets and bullfinches – but these payments now ceased.

The accounts contain frequent entries concerning the upkeep of the church; in 1639, in particular, there were expensive repairs when it was 'broken by a tempest'. At intervals it received a coat of whitewash, 'glew to season it' being added. Probably as a result of the 1639 storm, the church house was re-thatched in that year, at a cost of 16s. 6d. for 112 sheaves of reed. The rent of this building was one shilling a year. It is not clear whether the stock house and the church house were one and the same, but almost certainly they were. Money given in alms was often referred to as the church stock, the burial register records the deaths of aged poor men who have died in the stock house, and it was not uncommon for the church house of a parish to be used as a poor house.

In Dunster the accounts of the overseers of the poor show that in 1654 more than £250 was held for the benefit of the poor; it was lent out to various parishioners in

37. Old Dunster cottages in the 1920s.

small sums. Interest accruing resulted in a steady increase in the total amount available: more than £350 in 1662 and over £470 in 1713.

In the late 17th century seamen were still being captured by Mediterranean pirates. Dunster parish paid small sums to 'six seamen that were taken by the Turks', to a poor man 'that was redeemed out of Turkey', to two women who had lost £17 and whose husbands had been taken by the Turks, and so on. As in Minehead, sufferers from shipwreck were helped; in 1678, for instance, 1s. 6d. was given to some men and their families who had lost their ship and goods 'coming from Virginny going to Plymouth', while a Mr. Leigh and 10 seamen who had lost their ship on a voyage from the West Indies were also helped.

Until the end of the 17th century, Dunster's poor people were maintained in their own homes; their rent was paid and their clothes bought for them, and they received a weekly payment for their food. If they fell ill, medicaments and medical treatment were provided free. But in 1699 it was decided to house the poor in one building; the thatching of it cost 14 shillings for the reed, 1s. 3d. for spars and eight shillings to the thatcher. As with Minehead church house, the rent was a shilling a year.

In 1728 a public meeting was held in Dunster parish church at which it was agreed that there was to be a similar meeting 'on the first Tuesday in every Month about three of the Clock in the Evening duly to consider the affairs of the Parish, to hear the grievances of the Poor, and to view and examine the Overseers' monthly Accounts'. A very democratic proceeding, with no chance of sharp practice on the part of the overseers.

The poor were to be paid weekly on Fridays between 11 a.m. and 12 noon in the church; unless they were prevented by sickness 'or any other reasonable cause' they had to attend personally or forfeit that week's payment. They also had to 'frequent the Public Worship of Almighty God in the Church, as in duty bound', again on pain of forfeiting a week's payment for 'such sinful omission and neglect'. At least, as has been said, benches were provided in the church for them to sit on.

Until the early 18th century there does not seem to have been any medical man in attendance at the almshouse, although in 1678 a Dr. Handcock is mentioned as receiving two pounds for curing one of the inmates. Payments are made to a number of persons, both men and women, who have achieved cures of one or another of the poor people. In 1717, however, the accounts go into some detail concerning an amputation on a man referred to as Old Blake. In addition to his fee, ninepence was spent on beer for the doctor; rum to render the patient insensible might have been more merciful. Various items were bought for Old Blake; straw (by way of a bed?), four yards of cotton tape, as a bandage, possibly; even a neck of mutton to tempt his appetite. He was nursed by his daughter and another woman. Although a second doctor, named Cording, was called in, Old Blake did not survive. About twelve or fourteen shillings probably covered the expenses of his funeral; his shroud cost 4s. 8d., and at that time 'stretching forth' a body, swearing an affidavit, certifying death and digging a grave each cost a shilling, while the ringer of the funeral bell might receive two shillings and a further shilling or two might be spent on ale for the mourners.

Dr. Cording was later appointed to supply the poor of Dunster with 'Surgery and Physick as need shall require and at any distance within two miles of the same' at an annual fee of £5.

Overseers paid a premium with children bound out as apprentices. The payment varied, but was usually about one to two pounds. Indentures were kept in a chest in the chancel of Dunster church. A boy might be bound to a cordwainer, a weaver, a thatcher; a girl to a sempstress. Children of both sexes might be sent to work on private estates.

In 1766 there were 16 old people and 14 children in the Dunster poor house; in 1805 there were 38 inmates altogether. Accommodation was cramped. There were two bedrooms for women and one for men. Each room had three beds in it, and there was one more bed on the staircase. Not only does this imply that each bed was shared by three and perhaps often four people, but the bedding was scanty. A meeting of ratepayers reported that the sheets were not sufficient for cleanliness and there were no blankets, only rugs of some kind which were not considered 'sufficient of themselves to keep the elderly people warm'.

Minehead had established a parish workhouse by the 1730s, but for some reason – economy, perhaps – it was 'suppressed' in 1753 and its 28 occupants were sent out to receive outdoor relief of one to two shillings a week. It seems that the system was not satisfactory, and in 1756 the workhouse was re-opened. An inventory of 1772 shows how the building was furnished. The parlour had a table, a long form, two chairs, two stools and a 'brakeboard' for kneading dough. The hall had a table and four forms, two chairs, two stools and two iron heaters. In the kitchen were two boilers fixed in the wall, one wooden horse, sundry pails and tubs and earthenware bowls 'sufficient for the use of the house'. Sleeping accommodation seems to have been slightly better than at Dunster; in various parts of the house there were 26 beds, 24 bedsteads, 31 blankets, 26 sheets, 28 rugs and a dozen trunks or boxes. At the time there were 26 adults and 14 children there, so bedding was far from adequate.

Materials for the poor people's clothes were bought locally in quantity and made up as required. There were charges such as 'Making Sarah Nichols' coat and jacket, 1s. 6d.; Cullins' coat and breeches, 3s. 3d.' 'Bay' woollen cloth was 9d. a yard; serge 1s. 4d.; canvas ninepence three-farthings; blanketing 1s. 1d. Men's shirts cost 3s. each, and hose fourpence halfpenny a pair. Women's stockings were more expensive at from 8d. to 11d. a pair. In Dunster a cloth called Dowlas was bought, and another material caused spelling difficulties; it may be assumed that it was broad calico that came out as 'brod Calley Crow'.

Churchwardens' accounts in general offer a useful guide to the price of food, or at least the kind of food eaten by the poorer sections of the population, in the late 17th and the 18th centuries, and show that there was little increase in the price of such things as meat, butter, cheese, sugar, wheat and coal during the 18th century. Beef, mutton, pork and veal all remained somewhere between 2d. and 3d. a pound, butter 3d. or 4d., cheese 1½d. and sugar 5d. A bushel of potatoes cost 7d., of wheat around 4s. 6d., and of coal about 8d.

It was not until the Napoleonic wars that there was a sharp increase in the price of food, which in some places led to rioting. It is interesting to find in the Dunster churchwardens' accounts examples of an arrangement not uncommon during those wars; a man might pay for a substitute to serve in the Militia in his place. In consequence, the care of the substitute's wife and children might devolve upon the parish. Such entries as '1798. Paid to the wife of Nicholas Collard he sarveing in the Militia for William Moody, £1 15s.' and 'John Collards wife 45 weeks and child three weeks he sarveing in the Militia for William Staddon £2 8s.' appear.

Dunster's burial registers, like Minehead's, offer reminders that all too many voyagers lost their lives. In 1705, for instance, six seamen were buried there from one wreck, and 30 years later 19 soldiers, a boy, two women and two children were buried on a February day. The cost to the parish of this mass burial was just over £9. The victims were from the Bristol to Waterford packet *Lamb*, wrecked on Minehead beach; altogether 78 lives were lost in this wreck.[2]

Although by this time the tiny haven of Dunster must have finally silted up, the sea was always visible from the castle and the Tor and the hills around; no place so close to the coast could have quite forgotten its maritime past, or needed a disaster like the *Lamb* to remind it of its harsh realities.

*Chapter Nine*

# Eighteenth-century Minehead

A bird's eye view of Minehead, North Hill and Warren Point is reproduced by Hancock, who suggests that it was drawn when Colonel Alexander Luttrell was contemplating the new pier he began in 1704. It shows that the town had already developed that division into three parts, like Caesar's Gaul, on which visitors were to comment during the next 200 years: Higher Town (also called Upper or Church Town), Lower or Middle Town, and Quay Town. According to Savage, there were 124 houses in Higher Town in 1705, 130 in Lower Town and 64 in Quay Town, the total population being 1,800, but he supplies no reference for these figures, which sound improbably high.

Some thirty years later a survey of the Luttrell's manor of Minehead was taken.[1] This may have been on the orders of Colonel Alexander's son, another Alexander, towards the end of his short life of 32 years, or it may have been when he died in 1737, leaving considerable debts – very much as his uncle Colonel Francis Luttrell had done in 1690 – and his widow Margaret was holding the estate for her daughter the heiress, whose name was also Margaret.

It shows the names of the principal streets and some minor lanes: Bampton Street, Friday Street, Frog Street, Middle Street, 'New Street leading home to the Church', which later was to be destroyed by fire, Butts Lane, Fishers Lane, Heron Lane, Watery Lane. There were also Hangman's Lane and Petherton Lane, apparently reached by way of Falklands Court, where the Presbyterian Meeting House stood and which branched off from Middle Street.

The town was well supplied with public houses, with one or two in all the main streets. On the Quay were the *Lamb*, the *King's Arms* and the *New Inn*, with ale houses called the *Red Lion* and the *Star* in Quay Street. On the wharf at the end of Middle Street was the *Blue Anchor*. The Market Place had the *Royal Oak*, the *Rose and Crown* and the *George*; on the east side of Market Street was the *White Hart* and in the Old Market was the *Swan Inn*. In Bampton Street was the *White Horse*; in Frog Street, the *Angel*; in Friday Street a second *George Inn*. The Upper Town had another *Rose and Crown*. In Middle or Lower Town stood the *Plume of Feathers* which had belonged to the rectory. It was 'a very good house consisting of severall chambers and roomes, courts, backsides, orchards and gardens'. In 1727 Colonel Alexander II bought one-third of it, together with other property belonging to the vicarage. (It is remarkable that a list headed 'Victuallers and Voters' drawn up for Henry Fownes Luttrell before the parliamentary election of 1761 shows 13 inns, only two of which, the *Angel* and the *Lamb*, bear the same names as earlier licensed premises – and they were in different streets.)

The survey of *c.* 1737 shows that there were 209 tenants of the manor, holding 321 tenements. In the hamlets around the town – Periton, Woodcombe, Wydon, Hindon

– lay farms, most of them rather larger than the medieval smallholdings, though still not very big: from between twenty or thirty acres to just under eighty. Both East and West Myne were now single farms, not divided among several tenants as in the past. West Myne with North Ridge amounted to 141 acres. The largest holding in the manor was Higher Hopcott, extending to 424 acres, which included 300 acres of hill 'for pasturing sheep and cutting turf'. There were also Minehead Marshes, amounting to 80 acres divided among five tenants who paid a total rent of £82, and Minehead Common, which took in Minehead Hill, Periton Hill and North Hill. All customary tenants (i.e. every tenant of the manor who was bound to do suit at the lord's court, as in medieval times) were allowed to graze their sheep on the Common, dig turf and take heath and furze 'without denyall so it be for their own use'.

Dwelling houses varied considerably in their size and condition. On the one hand there was the Great House of Isett Quirk. She was probably the Isott [*sic*] Quirk who died in 1786, aged 90. The house opened on the harbour and contained a kitchen, a hall, a brewhouse, a buttery, 'a very good cellar against the hill, one other cellar on the west side of the house, a chamber over it, a large stable adjoyning, and nine chambers over the kitchen, hall, and other lowe rooms'. By contrast there was Joane Pearce's house, known by the name of Totterdown Castle, which stood (or had stood) under the hill behind the houses on the west side of the street leading to the harbour. This was 'decayed', and a note in the margin added 'buried by ye Rubbidge of ye Hill'.

The survey shows where various trades were carried on. That important building, the Town Mills, lay on the west side of Bampton Street; there were in fact two grist mills with their water courses drawn from the Bratton stream, a house, garden and mill-pond. Somewhere near the Quay was 'a dwelling house convenient for a White Baker, with a woodhouse and garden'. There were a number of what were known as Red Herring Houses, where the locally caught fish were smoked, large quantities of them for export. (According to Savage, 4,000 barrels a year were sent to Mediterranean ports.) Three of these smoke houses adjoined the *King's Arms*, a fourth had recently been built on waste ground behind the Quay, and a fifth, also new, stood in Butts Lane. A William Saffin held a tan yard in Watery Lane, 'with as much of the waste by the Pump there as can well be spared without annoying the Highway', and on the east side of New Street was a bark shop, its produce necessary for tanning, an industry which continued in Minehead until the end of the 1920s. In Higher Town lived a soap-boiler and a serge weaver; in Bampton Street Andrew Blake held a very good house with a dye house behind it; at Puddle Bridge, which crossed the Bratton stream, a glover held what sounds like a positive factory of 20 low rooms and chambers. The Common Pound lay at the top of Bampton Street, and attached to a dwelling in the same street, known as 'the house between the Arches' was a shop and outhouse called the Ivy House. There was still at least one Hemp Garden, described as at the higher end of Heathfield.

A number of public works were carried out during the decades around the mid-18th century. Yet more repairs were necessary to the pier after a great storm in 1741 so, only 25 years after the last rebuilding work, local masons estimated that yet another new wall nearly three hundred feet long and 16 feet high would have to be built. Twenty years later a new road was cut from Puddle Bridge to a point near the end of Quay Street, which Hancock says is no doubt the one which later led from Blenheim Gardens to the Quay. It was proposed that a toll house should be built to pay for this, to take money from strangers, not townspeople.

It was at about the same time that the Act of Parliament was obtained for improving the road from Minehead through Dunster and Timberscombe to Hele Bridge on the Exe; this was the road that ran – and indeed still runs – over Lype Hill, rising to nearly 1,400 feet above sea level. However in the 1740s travellers were still having to make their way by roads described as ruinous, narrow and incommodious. John Wesley, coming from Cornwall in April 1744, would have had to follow such roads, but nothing concerned him save his mission; having arrived in Minehead between five and six in the evening, he found a general expectation among the people that he would preach to them, and at once did so, near the shore. 'Most of the gentlemen of the town were there, and behaved with seriousness and decency', he noted, suggesting that gentlemen did not always do so. He crossed to Wales the next day, evidently enjoying excellent weather conditions, as his sloop 'ran over the Channel in about four hours'. He made a similar journey, and crossing, in July of the following year.

In about 1767 a free school was established in Minehead, probably, Hancock says, 'by the squire of the day', who would have been Henry Fownes Luttrell. (Margaret, the daughter of the Colonel Alexander Luttrell who died in 1737, married her cousin, Henry Fownes, in 1747; he added her name to his and took a keen interest in the Luttrell estates. Margaret, having borne him 10 children, died when she was only forty.)

The town seems to have had a school of some sort in the 17th and 18th centuries; in the churchwardens' accounts for 1655 there is an item showing six shillings being paid to a Robert Griffith 'for going to Taunton by Warrant concerninge Ministers and School Masters'. By about 1753 there is a reference to 'A School House and garden, formerly the Quakers' Meeting House and burial ground'. Possibly it was in this school that a John Thomas taught; he was referred to in the parish burial register as 'Schoolmaster' when he died in 1763.

The school set up in 1767 was for the instruction of 20 poor children, who were to be appointed by the founder, 'only one child of a family at one time'. A leaving age of 15 was stipulated – surprisingly late when it is considered that the leaving age decreed by the Education Act of 1870 was 13, or earlier in special circumstances. Whether the school at which John Thomas had been a master continued to exist, or was absorbed by the new one, does not appear. In general, it would seem that provision for the education of the poor in 18th-century Minehead was even more limited than in some other towns of comparable size, although there may have been one or two very small, unrecorded dame schools, where children might receive elementary instruction for a few pence a week.

In 1818 the House of Commons called for parochial returns concerning the education of the poor, and the vicar of Minehead reported that there was a free school supported by John Fownes Luttrell (the son of Henry) but that there was no endowed school in the parish. There was a Sunday school supported by private subscription, attended by 50 children, and several day schools attended by about a hundred. Savage comments that the poorer classes were 'totally unable themselves to educate their children, but are desirous of having them instructed'.

From the 1660s, in the Minehead burial register, the occupations of men are often entered (or the fact that they were gentlemen, and so of no occupation). As far as women were concerned, it was only noted if they were widows, servants, or had died in the poor house. As might be expected, many men earned their living from the sea: mariner, seaman, boatman or sailor appear frequently, and there were excisemen and land-waiters. Other occupations include butcher, carter, chandler, glazier, goldsmith, husbandman, labourer, mason, meadman, organist, porter, sexton, schoolmaster, sheergrinder, soldier and tailor. Few, apart from an occasional weaver or clothier, are now connected with the wool trade.

Despite the absence of wool imports, a considerable amount of what was known as 'bay yarn' continued to be brought in during the 1770s, together with linen cloth and large quantities of ox and cow hides, some lamb and goat skins, and a certain amount of butter, tallow and lard. During the late 1760s the average annual total of port duties on goods imported to Minehead, after deduction of all expenses, was £700.[2]

That herrings were still being caught, smoked and exported is noted by Benjamin Martin, writing in 1759; he speaks of mighty shoals of the fish coming up towards the Severn. He also mentions laver growing on the rocks near Old Cleeve; people gathered, cleansed and 'pickled' it, and 'sent it to a great Distance'. It had a pleasant taste, he thought, was nourishing and a good anti-scorbutic.[3] Some forty years later Billingsley observed that the herring fisheries of Minehead, Porlock and Watchet were all considerable; they provided the lower classes with a cheap and wholesome food, he said, especially as the duty on salt for curing fish had been taken off. He thought that the fishery should be promoted and encouraged to give employment during the winter to sailors who were busy in the limestone and culm trade in the summer.[4]

At about this time Collinson was noting that vessels belonging to the port carried alabaster; the cliffs two miles westwards abounded with fine alabaster. Early in the previous century Gerard had recorded the existence of local alabaster. A Dutchman had first found it, he said, and it was obtainable in a variety of mixed colours – pure white, white spotted with red or black, red spotted with white and 'a perfect black spotted with white'. It was much used for tombs and chimney pieces.

From 1786 until 1834 Minehead was a Registry Port; Watchet and Porlock were sub-ports, dependent on its Custom House. But after that time it was absorbed by Bridgwater.[5] In 1829 Savage was writing that the port's trade with the West Indies, Virginia and the Mediterranean was nearly at an end; there were only five or six vessels belonging to it, two of them carrying grain, malt, bark, timber, flour and some leather to Bristol and bringing back groceries, iron, etc. Others took flour, malt and timber to Wales, returning with the limestone and culm used in local kilns. Herring fishery had become a chancy business; the arrival of a considerable shoal was now very uncertain. He added that 'Great numbers of cattle, sheep and pigs are landed at Minehead every season, but the vessels which bring them in leave the port in ballast'. (The importation of cattle was no longer illegal.)

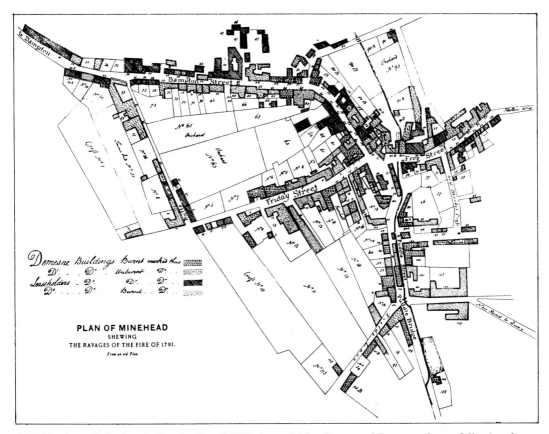

38. This plan of Minehead after the fire of 1791 shows Friday Street and Bampton Street following the same courses as they do today, but Holloway Street appears as Frog Street leading to Holloway, and Puddle Street is shown where the Avenue now lies. The Old Market Croft, Quirke's Almshouses and 'New Road to Quay' may all be noted (Hancock).

But as the older ways of earning a living gradually diminished, the first signs of the new industry that was to replace them here, as in so many seaside villages and towns, began to appear. A directory of about 1790, having remarked on Minehead's 'safe and commodious harbour', adds that the town 'was but little frequented otherwise until lately, but on account of the pleasantness of the situation and salubrity of the air, a number of persons of fashion have been induced to visit it as a bathing place in the summer season'.[6]

Unfortunately, in July of the following year, Minehead experienced a serious fire. According to the 'Annual Chronicle' of 10 July 1791, the miller in Bampton Street had been 'trying an experiment' by burning a tar barrel. It was an extremely unfortunate experiment. The day was windy, and the flames caught a nearby furze rick of the sort that many people then maintained in their yards as a fuel store. The fire spread rapidly to adjoining houses, most of which were thatched. Much of Quay Town and Middle Town were burned down: 'the centre of this once respectable and flourishing town is now become a heap of ruins', one writer remarked. Yet there was only one death, of a 'poor maniac' called Price; locked up, he was forgotten. Few if any of the houses were insured, and the total losses were estimated as about £18,000.

An undated circular, signed by Francis Fownes Luttrell and others, speaks of setting up two committees, one in Minehead and one in London, on the advice of 'several very respectable aldermen and gentlemen of the Common Council of London to petition that august body on behalf of the unfortunate sufferers by the late dreadful fire at Minehead'. (Perhaps it was recalled that at the time of the Great Fire of London more than a century earlier, Minehead parishioners had contributed to a fund for the 'distressed people' of the capital.) The circular claimed that half the loss caused by the fire 'falls upon the middling and lower orders', and that 73 houses, with out-houses, stables and so on, had been destroyed in a few hours. There had already been contributions; a local doctor named Brocklesby opened a subscription with £50. Altogether some £4,000 was collected, most of it coming from sympathisers in London.

Whether or not the fire had anything to do with it, the Rev. Richard Warner, making a walking tour in 1800, commented that those who had resorted to Minehead in the summer season for bathing, health and pleasure had deserted the place. Yet he saw much to attract visitors: 'the shore is hard and firm; the machines commodious; the lodgings reasonable; provisions cheap and plenty'. Moreover the turnpike roads to Bristol were excellent. Warner decided that the distance from the metropolis and the populous parts of England 'is sufficiently great to prevent those *felicity-hunters*, the teazing insects of fashion, from disturbing with their impertinent buzzings the pensive or rational pleasures of them who choose to enjoy nature at Minehead'.

Warner had followed the beach the whole way from Watchet ('a miserable stinking place') by way of Blue Anchor, then merely 'a neat little inn ... a small house for

39. Blue Anchor, five miles east of Minehead, as it was in 1853 (Rock).

lodgers' and a bathing machine. He made a brief detour to admire Dunster Castle's 'proud turrets' shooting up from a venerable wood, and its judiciously planned walks: he considered that the slope which 'unites its steep with the flat moor below is tastily managed and appropriately ornamented'. He dropped down to the shore again and went on over the long rabbit warren 'as thickly inhabited as a Chinese province'.[7]

He found the heights that divided the three parts of Minehead fatiguing. He stayed at the *Plume of Feathers*, which had either escaped the fire or been rebuilt. A good deal of rebuilding must have gone on, as he makes no reference to fire-blackened ruins or cleared spaces – yet it seems probable that there were fewer buildings than formerly, as he speaks of Quay Town as 'by far the most considerable of the three', which it certainly had not been before, if the 1783 figures quoted by Savage are correct: 98 in Higher Town, 141 in Lower Town and only 45 in Quay Town. Warner thought little of what he calls Upper Town; the only thing it had to recommend it was the view, whereas Middle Town had the convenience of the post office, lodging houses and shops.[8]

The directory published in the 1790s, already quoted, certainly exaggerated in estimating that the town had 'about 500 houses and 2,000 souls'; the number of inhabitants returned at the first national census of 1801 was 1,168. By 1821 there were 280 families in 258 inhabited houses, 106 of them employed in agriculture, 76 in trade, manufacture or handicraft, and 98 not included in either category. The total population by then was 1,239.

The fire of 1791 was not the only one the town suffered. Savage says that the Upper Town had sunk to little more than a few straggling houses, 'the principal collection of which is called Parsons Street; the street called New Street was burnt down about fifteen years since [i.e. *c.* 1814] and has not been rebuilt'.

It is strange that a writer who saw Minehead in 1813 presents a very different view of Quay Town from Warner's. Middle Town, nearly half a mile inland, had the air of a decent village, but there was only a lifeless stillness about the harbour, 'the more melancholy, as not being the natural inheritance of the place, but the consequence of desertion and decay'; in Quay Town 'the utter loss of trade and all spirit of speculation is mournfully exhibited in many ruins of blackened walls which still remain unrepaired'.[9]

Yet by the 1830s Middle Town was coming up in the world; it had 'the best houses and the most respectable shops', and the former Puddle Street had been renamed the Parade; in a line with the houses in the latter an elegant new market house had been built, Savage recorded. The old established *Plume of Feathers* now had a rival, the *Wellington*. Both were coaching inns. From the former, a coach left for Bridgwater at 7 a.m. on three days a week, returning on the alternate days, and from the latter a mail coach had just begun to run to and from Taunton, by way of Dunster, and this was 'a great accommodation to the inhabitants of Minehead and Taunton, as well as to those who live in the neighbourhood of the road on which it passes'. In Minehead, as in so many towns of the period, the bustle and horn-blowing of the daily arrivals and departures of the four-horse mail coaches must have offered a new air of importance.

There were also carriers' carts. One, owned by a John Nation, left for Bridgwater every Tuesday, and for Dulverton every Wednesday; another, owned by a John Wake, ran to Taunton every Tuesday. For those who wanted to travel or send goods by water, there were the *Duke of Wellington* and the *Ranger*, sailing every fortnight, while half a dozen vessels with such names as *Eliza*, *Friends* and *Blossom* crossed to South Wales, though Pigot's *Directory* noted that their times of sailing were uncertain.

The 1844 edition of Pigot included a mention of a railway, though it was still 23 miles away. The nearest station was Taunton, on the Bristol and Exeter Railway, but a special coach ran from 'Dunn's office' on Mondays, Wednesdays and Saturdays at 7 a.m. However, presumably some passengers wanting to catch a train on other days travelled to Taunton by the mail coach.

It was to be another 30 years before the railway arrived at Minehead itself. When it came, the three parts of the town gradually merged into one; as a writer remarked at the beginning of the 20th century, they were 'enmeshed together in an upstart network of new roads and uncharacteristic villas that might be in suburban London, rather than Somerset'.[10] At the same time the town began to rely increasingly on that industry which had seen its first small beginnings at the end of the 18th century, with the arrival of those few pioneer 'persons of fashion'. From that time on, Minehead was to pride itself on its attractions as a seaside resort.

### Chapter Ten

# *Minehead's M.P.s[1]*

Minehead's parliamentary history began in 1562, when Elizabeth I granted the borough its charter of incorporation and the privilege of sending two members to parliament. Although Thomas Luttrell was one of the first two members returned, during the next hundred years only three of his descendants represented the borough: John in 1586 and 1588, Thomas in 1625, and Alexander, who, by taking his seat in 1640, became a member of the Long Parliament. But from the Restoration until 1708, and from 1768 until 1832, a Luttrell of Dunster Castle held one of the seats. In fact at times both were occupied by Luttrells. And when not himself standing for election, the Luttrell of the day saw to it that candidates had his approval; it was an outstanding example of a pocket borough.

Apparently there were no disputed elections until Sir Jacob Bancks stood in 1698. Bancks, as has been said, married the widow of Colonel Francis Luttrell; he therefore represented the Luttrell interest. A John Sandford unsuccessfully petitioned against his being returned, objecting that he was a foreigner who had used 'undue means', including treating and bribery. Bancks was to represent Minehead for 16 years, during which time he was a benefactor to the town on all occasions – or so the inscription on the statue of Queen Anne which he presented claimed.

The borough's two constables, appointed by the Luttrells, were the returning officers, and at times they were accused of flagrant dishonesty. During George I's reign unsuccessful candidates more than once brought charges of illegal practices against them; on one occasion they were said to have declared that the preferred candidates would be returned 'if they had but five votes apiece'.

40. The statue of Queen Anne given to Minehead in 1719 by the Swedish-born Sir Jacob Bancks, who served in the British Navy and, having married into the Luttrell family, represented the town in parliament from 1698 until 1714.

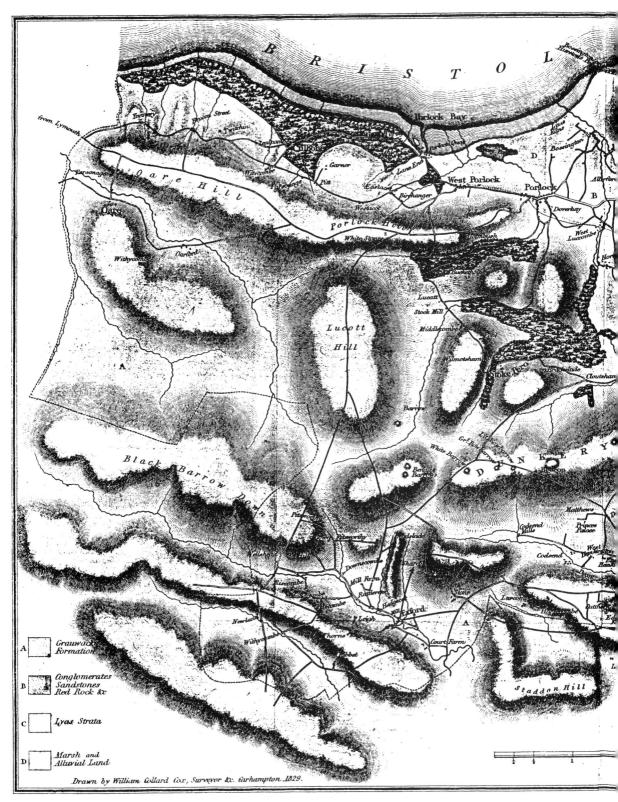

Drawn by William Collard Cox, Surveyor &c. Carhampton 1829.

41. This map was engraved in 1829, just three years before the Reform Bill of 1832 disfranchised Minehead and deprived the Luttrells of a safe parliamentary seat. Although prepared as a geological map, its interest today is largely in its clear delineation of the villages and small towns of west Somerset as they were at the time, and the network of roads connecting them. It shows that the first turnpike road from Dunster to Dulverton by way of Couple Cross and

A GEOLOGICAL Map of the Hundred of CARHAMPTON.

Printed by W Lander, Bristol

Sid.ᵗ Hall sculp.ᵗ

ᵈ by W. Strong, Bookseller, Bristol, & Exeter, Sept. 15, 1829, for Savage's History of Carhampton.

Lype Hill had already been superseded by a road following the route which was later to be upgraded into the A396.
Three turnpikes are marked: one on the approach to Dunster from Carhampton, another on the approach to
Timberscombe from Dunster, and a third at Wheddon Cross (Savage)

Throughout the 18th century bribery was commonplace, in Minehead as elsewhere. An agent for one of the candidates in 1734 noted that he had paid half-a-crown each to 272 voters, among them three inn-keepers, three mariners (one a Captain Coffin), two farmers, a ringer and a smith. Just 11 voters were set down as declaring themselves in favour of the candidate *without* receiving half-crowns.

In the election of 1755, Henry Fownes Luttrell was supporting a certain Henry Shiffner as one of the candidates, and was extremely annoyed at the outcome, for not only did Shiffner fail to get elected, but one of his followers was tried for bribery and convicted, in spite of the fact that Luttrell had 'taken care of ye jury' and so hoped that justice [*sic*] would be done. At the next election, in 1761, Shiffner was returned, with Lord Thomond, an Irish peer; it was on this occasion that the list headed 'Victuallers and Voters' was drawn up which provides the names of every inn and beer house in the town. Mr. Luttrell had seen to it that all prospective supporters of his candidate were lavishly entertained at the *Plume of Feathers*. The gentry were headed by Sir Thomas Dyke Acland and Mr. Luttrell; other guests included Mr. Mogridge, the vicar, four other parsons, three surgeons, 11 captains (of local vessels, not of naval or military rank), four customs officers and three excisemen, a roper, a glover and a soap boiler. Altogether 61 guests sat down to 'a whole buck, viz. a Haunch and Shoulder roasted, and the side pastied, a rump of beef boiled, greens, roots, Sauces, puddings etc at each table, also a Hare and two brace of Partridge and tarts at each table'.

The amount of alcohol consumed is not recorded, but it is probably on much the same scale as that supplied at a similar dinner 12 years later, when 85 guests downed about six gallons of brandy, six of rum, three dozen bottles of port and white wine, and 25 shillings worth of ale. These figures imply that each reveller, in addition to eating a large quantity of rich food, and drinking several glasses of port, consumed on average half a pint of rum and more than half a pint of brandy – to leave the ale out of account altogether.

Apart from large-scale entertainments, groups of about a dozen voters were invited to supper in various public houses: the *White Hart* in Friday Street and a second *White Hart* near Puddle Bridge, the *Anchor* and the *Ship*, both on the quay, the *Crooked Fish* in Middle Street, the *Carpenters' Arms* in Bampton Street, the *Three Horse Shoes* and the *Clothiers Arms*, both near Vicarage Gate, the *Halfmoon* in Puddle Street, the *Lamb* in Frog Street and several others known simply by the name of the licensee and the site: e.g. 'George Chapman's opposite ye Workhouse'. The guests at these suppers had venison, but their drinking was apparently limited to a guinea's worth of ale for the whole company. However, at 18th-century prices, this would have ensured that all had enough to make them drunk.

Whereas a vote could be bought for half-a-crown in 1734, the price rose sharply in the next 30 years. In 1767, when Henry Fownes Luttrell was a candidate, 30 leading townsmen who had turned down the offer of this sum were invited to dine at Dunster Castle, but many appear to have sent their excuses. It is interesting to find that the Rev. William Mogridge is not merely one of Mr. Luttrell's most fervent supporters, but is quite prepared to help in the business of bribery; through him, Hancock says, the various gifts to the voters were largely distributed. He wrote to his patron that he was willing to support his interests to the last penny, though the last penny was more likely to have been Luttrell's.

Merely bribing electors – especially as some of them had turned out to be incorruptible – was evidently considered not enough to ensure Mr. Luttrell's success. At one of those well-lubricated meetings at the *Plume of Feathers*, it was suggested that he should carry out a variety of improvements on his estate, such as building more houses, with good gardens, putting his cottages in good order, obtaining more weekly relief for certain poor persons who were begging from door to door (these would not have been eligible to vote, but helping them would have demonstrated the patron's philanthropy) and building a new market house.

The election took place in March 1768, and once again the voters were wooed with gallons of wine, ale and spirits, as well as gifts of beef and mutton. In cash, sums of between a guinea and five pounds were handed out, to a total of about £1,300 – a surprisingly large sum, in view of the small number of residents eligible to vote. They had to be 'parishioners of Minehead and Dunster who were householders in the borough of Minehead, not in the receipt of alms'. A *Directory* published in the 1790s estimated that such parishioners numbered 160, but this may be an underestimate: there had been 216 holders of tenements 30 years earlier, and by 1768 the total was probably about two hundred and fifty.

Henry Luttrell, having spent nearly £2,000 in all, was duly elected, with Charles Whitworth as his fellow M.P. Although Mr. Luttrell became unpopular in 1770 as a result of a Bill he applied for concerning the weighing of wool at the Town Hall, and a few townspeople tried to raise some opposition to him, he apparently had little difficulty in securing re-election in 1774. With his fellow candidate, his son John, he canvassed the town three times in August of that year and once more a few days before the poll. Sir Thomas Acland and some leading residents accompanied them. On election day the Luttrells led an impressive procession; at Alcombe Cross they were met by flag-bearers, drummers, fiddlers, 'Chamber Gun Men', the constables who would act as returning officers and a large gathering of voters of varying degrees of importance. At the head of these loyal followers they walked to Minehead market place, where the town crier called three times for silence, the constables were sworn in and – an ironic touch – the Bribery Act was read out. The Luttrells then offered themselves as candidates, polling took place at the Market House, and in due course Henry and John Luttrell were declared to have the majority of votes. They later claimed that they had not spent a penny on canvassing 'or in any other way on the voters'. Nevertheless, just five days before the election a list of all householders in the town had been taken, with notes on any repairs or alterations needed, and against the property of any uncooperative voter was entered 'Out with him when the time comes'. There was more than one way of securing votes in a pocket borough.

Soon after this Henry Fownes Luttrell, for some reason, applied for the Chiltern Hundreds, and a Thomas Pownall was elected in his place, with no nonsense about not paying for votes. An alphabetical list, dated 1775, divides voters into three classes: those few who would not accept five guineas; those who did accept; and those who would have opposed the candidate if not paid.

Savage remarks that the last contested election that succeeded against the Luttrell interest was in 1796. Supported by William Davis, a member of a Quaker family of

42. A view from Grabbist or Grabhurst Hill, looking out over Dunster as Mrs. Cecile Alexander, the prolific Victorian hymn writer, may have seen it when she wrote the words of 'All Things Bright and Beautiful' during a visit to the town.

Minehead merchants, John Langston was returned with John Fownes Luttrell. He spent a good deal of money in the town, building houses (22 of them at Woodcombe which were at first known as Langston's Town but later, when they were sold to Mr. Luttrell, as Botany Bay). He even built a ship, named after himself, and tried to promote local trade. However, he was not returned in the election of 1802, at which unlimited treating was offered at all the Luttrell inns. 'That Mr. Langston was treated with base ingratitude by many is certain', Savage admits, and gives an example. An elector was in prison for debt; Langston paid what the man owed and obtained his release. On his return to Minehead, the man promptly voted for Mr. Luttrell. Evidently some people could buy votes and some could not. Langston, who was in any case an Oxfordshire man, gave up, sold all his properties to John Luttrell and left. Savage evidently approved: 'The shadow of a contested election has never since appeared in Minehead, very much to the peace and quiet of the place and its neighbourhood'.

The Luttrells continued to hold one, and sometimes both, of the Minehead seats until the town was absorbed in the West Division of Somerset in 1833. Page says that when the John Fownes Luttrell of the time was given the news that the great Reform Bill of 1832 had passed, 'he clasped his head in his hands, exclaiming, in serio-comic tones, "Oh Mine Head! Mine Head"'.

He did not give in easily. With his agent, he prepared a long submission giving reasons why Minehead should be removed from the list of boroughs to be disfranchised, emphasising that Dunster Castle 'had once been the head of an extensive Honour, of which Minehead and other Manors within the two parishes, and a great number of other Manors in the county, were holden'. He proposed adding the parishes of Carhampton, Withycombe, Wootton Courtenay and Timberscombe to the borough, and seemed to contemplate a massive building programme of a sort that would have been a forerunner of the New Towns and Overspills of the 1950s and 1960s; there were, he said, 'facilities for building for the whole two miles between it (Minehead) and the town of Dunster on the east, and for nearly two miles to the boundary of the parish on the west: and that portion of the borough which is within the parish of Dunster might be very considerably extended in every direction'. Finally, although the trade with the West Indies had ceased some fifty years earlier, he spoke vaguely of the possibility of maintaining commerce with the islands.

None of this cut any ice with Lord John Russell. Minehead had been one of the most blatant examples of the pocket boroughs which he had determined to disfranchise, and he can have had no sympathy with arguments seeking to make it an exception.

*Chapter Eleven*

# A Growing Resort

The neighbourhood of Minehead, in 1830, was described as 'very picturesque and beautiful, being a continued succession of lofty hills, the sides of which are ornamented by patches of furze and coppice; the valleys are rich in pasture and agriculture; and a few miles to the westward the country is highly romantic, and affords fine subjects for the pencil; this fine scenery, together with good accommodation for bathing, annually draws a number of visitants [*sic*], to the emolument of the inhabitants'.[1]

A guide brought out by the town itself in 1857 remarked that recently several new houses had been built and 'here and there an attempt at improvement has been made, and during the Summer Season visitors, in search of health, begin to appear from Bristol, Cheltenham, Wales and even London'. There were one or two lodging houses with splendid views in Upper Town; moreover, rather surprisingly, most of the houses in Quay Town were said to be for the occupation of visitors during the season, as though they were the holiday homes of the late 20th century. One of the walks recommended was to Greenaleigh Farm, westwards under the shadow of North Hill. This had a room set apart for visitors where 'refreshment may be obtained of

43. A view of Minehead church in about 1908 (Harper).

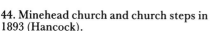

44. Minehead church and church steps in 1893 (Hancock).

45. A view of St Michael's church, Minehead, and North Hill, in 1853, sketched, perhaps, in Middle Street (Rock)

delicious brown bread and butter or native cream, or tea, if required, and the charge most moderate'. Greenaleigh was to continue to cater for holiday makers for many years. In the 1880s it was said by Page to be 'devoted to the high revel of junketing parties' when junketing had a literal meaning; 'groups of happy excursionists discussing that delicious admixture of syllabub and clotted cream for which the West Country is so justly famed' sat at tables in the open air. Until well into the 20th century the farm kept up its reputation for teas, lunches and junket and cream. It is now the property of the National Trust.

To the east, the Warrens still formed 'a pleasant level walk of turf, and the numerous inhabitants of the burrows when feeding of an evening afford a most amusing sight. On the sands there are generally a couple of bathing machines for the Ladies'.

Water Lane had been much improved; formerly it had been scarcely passable by ladies 'on account of the cattle in the way, and the flowing of the water', but, encouraged by an anonymous 'spirited individual', the inhabitants had got together and paid for it to be converted into an excellent road from the sea to the Parade.

Like other towns eager to attract holiday makers, Minehead impatiently awaited the arrival of the railway. The line from Taunton had reached Watchet by 1862, and an extension to Minehead was authorised in 1865. As the Minehead Railway Company failed to proceed, a new Act had to be obtained. This done, the first sod was cut at Minehead in December 1871, but it was July 1874 before the single line from Watchet, a little over eight miles of broad gauge, was completed, with two more

46. A view of Minehead harbour and North Hill in 1853 (Rock).

stations, at Blue Anchor and Dunster. Like so many on the line, Dunster station was at some distance from the place it served.

The official opening was reported in the *West Somerset Free Press*, the weekly newspaper that the local printers, Cox, Sons and Co., had first brought out in 1860. Tribute was paid to George Fownes Luttrell, one of the directors of the branch line, who had helped to hurry things forward. 'The result of his enterprise is the railway of today, with all its benefits and conveniences', the *Free Press* declared, adding that 'Minyarders devoted the day to a public holiday' and 'evinced much *esprit de corps*'. (Minehead was commonly pronounced *Minyard* at this time, according to Murray's *Handbook for Wilts, Dorset and Somerset*, published in 1859).

The usual sort of decorations for a 19th-century public celebration were put up in the streets – greenery twined round lamp posts, flags and banners and floral arches bearing slogans. Only one, 'God Speed the Train', sounds strictly relevant to the occasion. Another countered with 'God Speed the Plough' (did local agricultural interests have their doubts about railway transport?). Contemporary pious patriotism offered 'God Save the Queen'. A fourth archway possibly showed a touch of satire, bearing in mind the town's long wait for a link to the railway network: 'Time works Wonders', it said, while a fifth, with vague benevolence, advised 'Be Merry and Wise'. At Alcombe two more arches wished 'Success to Minehead Railway' and 'Thanks to G. F. Luttrell, Esq.' Minehead church bells rang, and jollifications included lunch in a tent in a field near the new station, a brass band concert and tea for schoolchildren.[2]

Early trains were not fast: the 9 a.m. from Paddington reached Minehead at 3.50 p.m., while the 11.20 a.m. express from Minehead arrived at Paddington at 6 p.m. Ten years later there were nine trains a day from Paddington to Taunton, but only four connected to Minehead. The 9 a.m. was now a little faster, reaching Minehead at 3.10, but other trains might take between seven and eight hours to do the journey. In the years immediately before the First World War the service speeded up considerably. In 1912, for instance, an express from Paddington to Minehead took 4 hours 17 minutes.

Passengers brought by the trains were not always welcome; some introduced a rowdy element to the town. When a works outing from the Bristol Wagon Works, 800 strong, arrived only a couple of weeks after the railway's opening, they rioted through the streets, stealing, fighting and breaking into gardens, the *Free Press* reported.

In the same year, 1874, excursionists were also arriving by sea, as they had been for at least ten years. In its early years the *Free Press* contained advertisements of R. S. Date's 'fine, fast Clyde-built Passenger Steamer, *Defiance*'. She left Watchet at 9.30 a.m., Minehead at 10.15 a.m. and Ilfracombe at 5.30 p.m. The return fares were three shillings for a fore cabin and four shillings for the saloon. By 1874 Date was running excursions from Watchet and Minehead to Cardiff and Swansea as well as Ilfracombe; the vessel he now used was 'the favourite, fast and well-known steamer, the *John Bewick*'. The West Somerset Mineral Railway issued cheap excursion tickets in connection with the steamer trips. Several trains a day carried passengers from Watchet to Comberow; a newspaper recommended the six-mile journey to those who were in need of 'a little pleasurable excitement, fond of beautiful scenery and partial to novel sensation'.[3] (This railway had been built to carry iron ore from the mines on the Brendons, and was completed as far as Comberow in 1861. It was opened to passengers in 1864. Even after the mines ceased working in 1879, two passenger trains a day ran until 1898.)

Those who wanted to travel westwards along the coast from Minehead could of course walk or hire a horse or carriage, but most visitors probably chose to use the public coaches. Even in winter there was a coach once a week to Lynton and Lynmouth and three times a week to Porlock. In summer it ran to all three places every weekday. A coach called the *Wild West* left for Dulverton every Tuesday, Thursday and Saturday from 22 June to 18 September; it connected with G.W.R. trains at Dulverton station. From Williton, coaches with such names as *Defiance* and *Accommodation* travelled to Minehead by way of Dunster.

After the First World War, when a service of what were then known as motor char-a-bancs had come into operation, a guide book observed that 'For those to whom speed is not a desideratum, the best way of seeing the country is from the top of the picturesque four-in-hand coaches which make trips during the season to Lynton and Lynmouth and other places of interest in the district'. These were the *Lorna Doone* and the *Red Deer*; when they were withdrawn, motor vehicles bearing the same names replaced them. Hobbs and Co. of Minehead were still advertising horse char-a-banc trips to a variety of places, from Dunkery to Cleeve Abbey, in the early 1920s.

Hotel accommodation was rapidly increased after the arrival of the railway. West of the station a large new hotel, the *Metropole*, was built in 1893, as well as 'a terrace of lodging houses commanding a fine view of the sea'. Wonson's *Beach Hotel* announced that it was 'pleasantly situated within 100 yards of the Sea, commanding extensive Views of the Bristol Channel, the Welsh Coast, etc., and also near the principal meets of the Devon and Somerset Staghounds and Mr. Luttrell's Foxhounds. Good stabling with loose boxes for hunters'.

Although for a time in the 1880s the *Wellington*, built in 1820, was referred to as the 'Wellington Coffee Tavern', offering apartments 'at very reasonable charges', it changed to the

47. The Clock Jack in Minehead church (Harper).

*Wellington Temperance Hotel* not long afterwards; it was pulled down and rebuilt in 1893. By 1904, when it had become the headquarters of the West Somerset Polo Club, it was simply the *Wellington Hotel* and, like the *Beach Hotel*, stressed its convenience for meets of the Staghounds, the West Somerset and Exmoor Foxhounds and the Harriers. The *Plume of Feathers* called itself the *Feathers Hotel* (T. Thristle, proprietor) and claimed that 'This old-established Family and Commercial Hotel is well known for its ample accommodation, its comfort and the attention paid to visitors and others. Post horses and stabling; carriages to meet every train'.

It was reported in the *Minehead and West Somerset Advertiser and Visitors' List* that the lord of the manor (George Luttrell) had recently been constructing walks and drives on the south side of North Hill 'which enabled persons of delicate constitution to visit the hill in carriages'.

As its title indicates, the *Visitors' List* was intended for holiday makers. It was brought out by Samuel Cox at the *West Somerset Free Press* offices every Tuesday, price one penny. At first a four-page paper, it soon doubled to eight pages. It included articles on local history and places of interest, coach and railway timetables and fares and details of church and chapel services, as well as 'Bits from Books', a 'Letter for Ladies', short stories and some verse. No doubt one of its main attractions, as far as visitors were concerned, was that it offered a medium in which they could have the satisfaction of seeing their names printed. The paper listed those staying, not only

48. Minehead in 1893, showing North Hill still an open space except for a disproportionately large Elgin Tower. The esplanade has not yet been built. The *Beach Hotel* is in the left foreground and the station is busy (Jeboult).

at main hotels, but at lodging houses in the Avenue, the Parade, Wellington Square, Bampton Street, the Parks, Blenheim Road and Blenheim Terrace, Quay Street and Station Terrace. Visitors to places outside Minehead – Dunster, Porlock, Blue Anchor, Watchet and Lynmouth – were also included.

Minehead had several fair-sized department stores which advertised in the paper. There was Bond's West Somerset Stores at No. 2, The Parade, with grocery, drug and drapery departments; at No. 2, Park Street were Treweeke Brothers, general drapers, dress-makers and milliners, who also ran a grocery and provision department and a tea warehouse. The latter 'begged to call attention of Visitors to their large and well-assorted stock of dress fabrics, amongst which will be found choice designs in French Sateens and Zephyr Check Cambrics suitable for seaside wear. Costumes made to order from 18s. 6d. to 35s. Bathing requisites of every description. Special line in sunshades for sea-side, and straw hats from sixpence three-farthings to one shilling and sixpence three-farthings'.

And in July 1883 a 'Notice to Visitors' called attention to the fact that 'Floyd and Co., Ready Money Drapers, Wellington Square, supply all the latest novelties in Millinery and Drapery Goods at City prices. Please note the address, opposite the New Church'. Isaac Floyd, who had been born in Porlock in 1851, originally opened his draper's shop in Friday Street in 1877. Floyd's celebrated their centenary in 1977, but closed a few years later. The building, which bears an official street name plate, 'Floyds Corner', was converted in the mid-1980s into a number of small commercial units.

Another shop in 19th-century Minehead belonged to the printer, Samuel Cox. His Bazaar and Library sold local photographs, albums of panoramic views, what were called 'view articles' in satinwood or fernwood, sketching materials, Berlin wools, fancy crewel work, toys, games and newspapers.

During this second half of the 19th century the population of the town nearly doubled, from 1,542 in 1851 to 2,782 in 1901; consequently much building went on. Those who could afford it bought up plots in the Avenue, the Parks and on North Hill to build what were described as villas. That strange house, the Elgin Tower, was built in the late 1880s and was not approved of by some writers on Minehead. Page, writing his *Exploration of Exmoor* in 1890, remarked on the 'heavy-looking castellated house, bran-new [*sic*] and rather out of keeping with the quiet beauty of the scenery'. Page did not care for what he called 'that civilisation whose ruthless pioneer is the locomotive, and whose sapper and miner that much-to-be-abused gentleman, the speculative builder'. He regretted the loss of the paved pathway from Quay Town to the church, much of it destroyed to make way for 'new roads and newer buildings'. He regretted that the 'shady repose' of New Road was now disturbed on summer days by trippers arriving at the station. He regretted the disappearance of Watery Lane, that once led from the tanyard to the sea, under the Avenue with its 'modern villas'. (In the Minehead of today, Watery Lane is the name given to the road running from Parks Lane to the junction of Hemp Gardens and Middle Street.)

That Minehead still retained most of its former charm, Page considered, was due to 'the good taste of the ground landlord and his agents'; it still belonged almost entirely to the Luttrells. Twenty years later, Charles Harper was less complacent; it was distressing, he said, to find the noble hill (North Hill) 'studded with villas and

49. The Avenue, Minehead, lying traffic-free and strangely deserted in the sunshine of
c.1905.

scarred with roads ... But a few years since, and here you had a scattered, unspoiled village. Today, by favour of the Luttrells, who own the land, and because the railway is handy ... the builder is walking, splay-footed, all over it, and hotels have arisen on the front, and there is a bandstand, there are seaside entertainers, and there are pickpockets among the crowds being thus entertained'.[4]

Increasing numbers of children had made the little free school built in 1767 quite inadequate. In 1866, a year before he died, Henry Fownes Luttrell, namesake and grandson of the original benefactor, commissioned Piers St Aubyn to design 'a handsome Gothic building' to offer education to 220 boys and girls. Luttrell generosity thus ensured that Minehead possessed a large new school for its poorer children three years before the Education Act of 1870.

In parishes all over Victorian England, new churches and chapels – Anglican, Nonconformist, Roman Catholic – were being built to accommodate rapidly growing congregations. Minehead was no exception. A Baptist Chapel, built in 1831, was enlarged in 1902; a Wesleyan Chapel in the Avenue, built in 1877, was enlarged in 1886, and a Roman Catholic church, built in Alcombe Road in 1896, was enlarged in 1900. The wife of the Rev. A. H. Fownes Luttrell, vicar of St Michael's from 1832 until 1899, provided a new church in 1880 in Wellington Square (this was the church referred to in Floyd's advertisement). Built and endowed entirely at her own expense, it was dedicated to St Andrew. At this time St Michael's itself had been neglected and was thought to be in danger of collapse. A fund was raised, to which George Fownes Luttrell contributed over £1,500, and Piers St Aubyn was called in. According to a guide to the church published in 1977, he approached his task with

50. 'The last days of sail'. Basil Kennelly identified these vessels, lying in Minehead harbour in about 1900, as the ketches *Thistle* and *Lively*, with the smacks *Sophia*, *Mary Anne*, *Pioneer* and *Ranger*.

51. The Parade, Minehead, in about 1905. The Market House, surmounted by its clock, had been rebuilt in 1902, only a year or two before this photograph was taken. It then had council rooms and a surveyor's office on the first floor.

ruthless thoroughness, removed the old wagon roof, altered windows, ripped out old pews and stones paving the floor, making it difficult to picture the interior as it had been before 1896.

However, contemporaries probably approved his work, and a company next requested him to design a new Town Hall, incorporating a concert hall to seat 550people. He died before the building was completed in 1889, in stone, at a cost of £4,000. The stone used was the attractive red sandstone that may be seen in a number of small towns and villages in Somerset. The same stone appears in the Exmoor Masonic Hall of 1889 and the Church Institute (formerly Young Man's Institute) of 1895, both in Bancks Street, in the Lifeboat House of 1901 and in a number of private houses of about the same period.

By now the town was lighted by gas; gas works had been built to the west of the harbour. A solicitor, Thomas Ponsford, former steward and legal adviser to the Luttrell estate, had much to do with this and other undertakings, including the formation of a water company to provide what visitors were assured was a 'soft, pure and ample' supply. When Minehead's Local Government Board became the Minehead Urban District Council under the provisions of the Local Government Act of 1894, with nine members, Ponsford was it first chairman. Later, he and his partners were involved in a scheme to introduce electric light. As solicitors to the promoters, they began to sound out local opinion in 1901, and as this was found to be favourable, the Minehead Electricity Supply Company was formed in 1903 and built works in Quay Lane.

One change resulting from the Local Government Act was the division of the original civil parish of Minehead into two, Minehead and Minehead Without. The former, of 603 acres, comprised the Urban District, and the latter, of 3,320 acres, was the remainder of the ancient parish. In 1916 the Urban District was to be considerably enlarged, taking in Alcombe from Dunster as well as part of Wootton Courtenay and Minehead Without. Alcombe soon became a suburb of Minehead, and Ponsford was commemorated in the name of a road running out towards Alcombe Cross.

By the late 1880s Minehead harbour was said by Page to be deserted except for a few small coasters. Three ship owners were still trading – John Crockford, Henry Pulsford and Alfred Wedlock, all of Quay Town. Some ten years later Hancock listed eight owners of small vessels, from W. J. Webber's *M and E* of 18 tons and Pulsford's *Ranger* of 14 tons, to E. J. Parkin with his *Flying Foam* of 84 tons: none of them any larger than their predecessors in Tudor times.

T. K. Ridler, who imported not only coal from Wales but a variety of builders' supplies, owned three little coasters. The smallest of these, the *Looe*, named after the Cornish village in which she had been built, was a striking example of the long-lasting properties of some of these tiny wooden ships: she had been sailing since 1787. She was to survive until 1905, when she was badly damaged in a storm, beached at Minehead and broken up. His *Periton*, by contrast, had been built on Minehead beach as recently as 1881; she was sunk in the First World War. His third coaster was the *Orestes*.[5]

But as R. S. Date had shown with his steamers *Defiance* and *John Bewick*, the time had come for a new kind of vessel carrying a new kind of profitable cargo, the sea-going day tripper. In the 1880s brothers named Peter and Alec Campbell, who had been running paddle steamers on the Clyde, moved to Bristol with their *Waverley*, which they claimed had been known as the Clipper of the Clyde. She was so successful as an excursion steamer that the Campbells soon ordered a new saloon paddler, the *Ravenswood*. By the 1890s their White Funnel Fleet had seven ships running trips to places along both coasts of the Bristol Channel, including Ilfracombe, Clovelly, Lundy, Swansea and Cardiff.

Although the Campbells were prepared to let their steamers lie off Clovelly and Lundy and put passengers ashore in small boats, for some reason they did not do this at Minehead when it was found that they could not conveniently lie alongside the old pier. It must have been galling for the people of Minehead to see the majestic steamers sailing to and fro, ignoring them. What was needed was a place at which passengers could be landed at any state of the tide. In 1899 a company was formed to set about building a 700-foot promenade pier at a cost of £12,000. Jutting out at an angle from the root of the stone pier, it was described as 'a light, strong structure, resembling in the distance a spider's web spun in the shelter of the quay, which effectually hides it from the sea front; it runs out into deep water and, emerging as it does from the shelter of the North Hill, makes an excellent promenade, affording bracing breezes at the extremity. A little trolly for carrying luggage to and from the steamers runs on a rail up the centre'.

52. Minehead Promenade Pier, built in 1890 at a cost of £12.000. It was demolished early in the Second World War as part of coastal defence measures.

The pier was opened by George Fownes Luttrell, to general rejoicing, at the end of May 1901; the opening was followed by a celebratory luncheon at the *Hotel Metropole*, attended by local notables. Charles Harper, characteristically, did not approve: 'the queer old Custom House has been wantonly destroyed to make an approach to a pleasure pier built in an impossible situation', he complained. However, the Campbell brothers did not consider that the pier was in an impossible situation. It had four landing stages to suit all states of the tide, and this 'placed this pleasant watering place and health resort within reach of passengers by steamer'.

Even before the official opening of the pier, Campbells announced that they would begin their cross-Channel service between Barry and Minehead on 20 May, in preparation for Whitsun week. They were soon running a daily service of their 'magnificent saloon steamers' between Minehead and Cardiff daily in summer, and to Ilfracombe and other places on the north coast of Devon several times a week, bringing in hundreds of passengers on every trip.

In Victorian times many resorts regarded it as desirable to have a tidy, level sea-front; the word esplanade became fashionable. It was not until the beginning of Edward VII's reign that Minehead constructed this embellishment for itself. Protected by a new sea wall, it ran westwards from the railway station towards the harbour.

53. The chapel of St Peter, built in 1910 in the outer of the two cellars left by Robert Quirke in 1630 for the maintenance of his almshouses. The room above was originally a reading room.

After the wreck of the *Forest Hall* in 1899 when, as has so often been described, the Lynmouth lifeboat was hauled by road to be launched at Porlock, local people began to ask why Minehead had no lifeboat. An appeal was made to the R.N.L.I.; George Luttrell donated a piece of land lying between the Pier Hotel and the gas works, exactly opposite the place where the new pier was being built, and a Miss Leicester of London offered a sum of money. As a result, Minehead acquired, in 1901, a sturdy lifeboat house in red sandstone. It was served by a pulling and sailing boat, the *George Leicester*, which remained in use until 1927. Her successors have been the *Hopwood*, the *Arthur Lionel*, the *Kate Greatorex* (the latter Minehead's first motor-driven lifeboat) and the strangely named *B.H.M.H.*, identified only by the initials of the four friends who donated her. Today the station, which is often open to visitors in summer, has a D-class lifeboat. The building is no longer neighboured by the gas works; open beach – Robert Quirke's 'chezell' – stretches westwards towards Greenaleigh.

When the *Pier Hotel* – now renamed *The Old Ship Aground* – was built, the inner of the two cellars given by Robert Quirke in 1630 for the support of his almshouses was demolished. For many years the outer cellar still belonged to the parish, and lay derelict. It seemed to the Rev. Francis Etherington, who became vicar of St Michael's in 1899, that good use might be made of the ancient bequest; he urged that it should be converted to a seamen's chapel. In 1910 this was done, the dedication being to St Peter.

Outside this chapel a panel headed 'God Speed the Ship' bears the names of the six men of Quay Town who died in the First World War and the seven who died in the Second. Inside, the floor slopes down, so that at the altar it is several feet below the street level outside. On the wall hangs a framed account of the traditional but somewhat unconvincing story that Robert Quirke vowed to build his almshouses when he and his brother were caught in a fierce storm at sea, and that on their safe return they sold ship and cargo to provide the funds. The beams, which may be supposed to belong to the original cellar, suggest that they came from some very old ship.

A recent painting by a local artist acts as a reredos. It represents Jesus walking on the waters of Minehead harbour towards a small sailing ship; this, a notice explains, is the *Emma Louise*.

The *Emma Louise*, 66 tons, was built in Barnstaple in 1883. Her owner, for the last 25 years of her working life, was also her captain, Philip Rawle, who had been skipper of T. K. Ridler's *Orestes* when he was only 20 years old, and who for 17 years was harbour master of Minehead; he died in 1972. In the 1950s he told Grahame Farr that there was no longer the profit in the coal cargoes carried by the *Emma Louise* to justify spending the large sum needed to repair her; not long afterwards she was sold. Yet it is fitting that a representation of Minehead's last sailing coaster should remain in this seamen's chapel on the quay.

54. The town arms of
Minehead adopted in the
1890s.

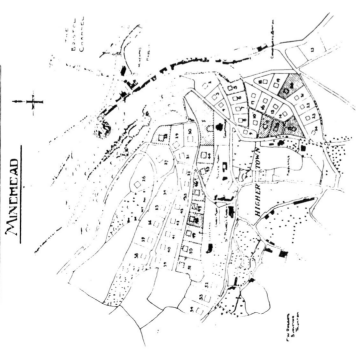
55. An advertisement for the development of North Hill in 1901 (Larter).

*Chapter Twelve*

# Twentieth-century Change

During the brief peaceful period between the death of Queen Victoria and the outbreak of war in 1914, Minehead continued to grow. Only six years after the Urban District Council had taken over the water supply and increased it, drawing from sources on Luttrell land at Periton, Woodcombe, Broadwood and Longcombe into a reservoir on the southern slope of North Hill, it was found that there were shortages during the holiday season. It was not only that there were many more residents in the town, and more visitors: there were more horses, all needing water. Owing to stag-hunting and what was called the increase in posting (horse and vehicle hire) required by 'a large pleasure-seeking community, every summer sees an enormous number of horses stabled in the town, quite out of proportion to the size of the place', observed the *West Somerset Free Press* in August 1910. Even the horses were not the end of it; that new form of transport, the motor car, used water. Cars had to be washed down, especially after travelling over the dusty roads of the time. The Council was doubtless grateful that, shortly before his death, George Luttrell gave them permission to search for a new gathering ground at Longcombe.

Beginning each spring, paddle steamers brought thousands of day trippers to the town, and carried those staying there on excursions to places on the Welsh or Devon coasts. The Campbells for a time had rivals: the Red Funnel Fleet belonging to the Barry and Bristol Steamship Company began to run trips to and from Minehead. In 1910 they announced a special outing to Weston, Penarth and Cardiff, timed to enable passengers to see Captain Scott's *Terra Nova* 'as she leaves Britain's shores'.

On land, horse-drawn vehicles were facing competition; not long after the accession of George V no fewer than four Minehead garages were advertising motor char-a-banc trips 'to places near and far', although in fact the most distant was not so very far: it was Taunton.[1]

While the majority enjoyed their organised outings, a minority played the elitist game of polo. The West Somerset Polo Club was thriving. Founded in 1898, at first it used the firm sands of the beach for matches, on which race meetings, too, were often held. When Minehead's seven-acre Recreation Ground was opened the following year, the club was able to make use of part of it. In Edwardian days

56. Equestrian sports were of great importance in the Minehead of the 1920s (Guide Book, 1920s).

57. The emphasis once again on equestrian and other sports (Guide Book, 1920s).

matches were played at a ground at Newbridge, halfway between Porlock and Allerford. 'Few prettier or more picturesque spots could have been selected than this meadow beside the babbling Horner Brook', one writer remarked.[2] However, George Luttrell's son Alexander provided a new ground for the club, a levelled space below Dunster Castle known as the Lawns. Each summer matches were played every Wednesday and Saturday at 3.30. A brake was run from the *Plume of Feathers* to carry spectators (admission sixpence, teas available). An annual tournament was held in August, with several visiting teams competing.

But the late summer of 1914 put an end to polo for some time; the young officers who had taken part in the matches and tournaments were soon on active service. The paddle steamers stopped running. Requisitioned for use by the Navy, they sailed away to become minesweepers and patrol boats. The Campbells' *Barry* was sent out to the Dardanelles to carry ammunition and stores, and when British troops were forced to withdraw, was the last vessel to leave Suvla Beach, taking the beachmaster and rearguard with her. Two other Campbell steamers were lost: both the *Brighton Queen* and the *Lady Ismay* were blown up by mines.

In Victorian times, Minehead was the headquarters of the 2nd (Prince Albert's) Volunteer Battalion of the Somerset Light Infantry, and often played host to Volunteer Brigades, which held their summer camps on North Hill by permission of the Luttrells. In July 1898, for instance, the *Minehead Advertiser and Visitors' List* reported that the town had 'all the rush and bustle of a garrison town. Redcoats gleam upon every highway and bye-way. Against the sombre hue of the dark green Gloucesters and the granite grey of the Somersets, the brilliant scarlet of the Welsh comes out in showy prominence'.

In July 1905, the 4th Battalion Volunteer Brigade of the South Wales Borderers crossed the Bristol Channel in one of the Red Funnel Fleet's steamers and disembarked at the promenade pier. Marching along the Quay and up the long winding way to camp, they must have taken the minds of the onlookers back to the Boer War, which had ended just three years earlier. Yet at the same time they may have seemed to be playing at soldiers; the idea of another war, longer, far more ferocious and so much closer to Britain, might have seemed an improbable horror to holiday-makers in their tranquil Edwardian summer.

The edition of the *Free Press* which appeared on the day war broke out, 4 August 1914, had been printed too soon for the news to be included, but the issue for 11

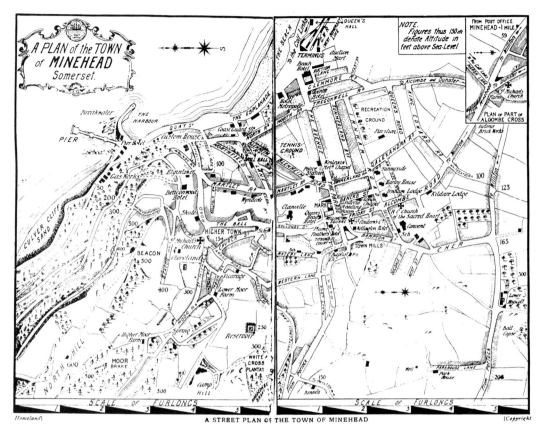

58. Map of Minehead from a Guide Book of the 1920s.

August carried a headline 'The Great War'. This was the phrase that virtually every British newspaper, from the national dailies to the provincial weeklies, seized on from the outset.

In this year the 5th Somerset Territorials (the former Volunteer Brigades had by now become the Territorials) were in camp on Salisbury Plain, and the *Free Press* reported that men were joining the regular army from the camp. In Minehead a public meeting was held to appeal for recruits. Of those who hurried to join in those early weeks of the war, or joined later, or were conscripted after 1916, more than a hundred did not live to come home to Minehead. The town's memorial to them, a cross of grey granite, was put up in Martlet Road, almost opposite the Elgin Tower; its base bears 104 names. On the seaward side is a granite seat; above it are inscribed the names of the 54 men who died in the Second World War.

In spite of shortages and restrictions, civilians did not stop taking holidays during the war, but no seaside resort could expect to be as busy as it had been in peace time, and all those on the Bristol Channel coasts missed the summer crowds of seaborne trippers, and welcomed their return when surviving ships of the Campbells' White Funnel Fleet, new paintwork replacing their drab war-time colours, reappeared for

59. The bathing beach, Minehead, and a view of North Hill, in about 1909.

60. The Minehead and West Somerset (Luttrell Memorial) Hospital. Originally designed as a new Town Hall by Piers St Aubyn, the building was completed in 1889 at a cost of £4,000. The First World War saw its conversion into a hospital.

the August Bank Holiday of 1919. The Yellow Funnel Fleet of W. H. Tucker of Cardiff offered competition for a year or two; then Campbells were able to buy them out and, having acquired their paddlers *Lady Moyra* and *Lady Evelyn*, renamed them *Brighton Queen* and *Brighton Belle*. (Brighton was the headquarters of the Campbells' other excursion steamer enterprise, which served a number of south coast resorts.) Finally they bought Minehead promenade pier for £2,500; the company that ran it had inevitably suffered losses during the war years.

Minehead's population was still growing rapidly, even allowing for the fact that in 1916 it had taken in Alcombe and parts of other parishes. From 2,782 in 1901, it had risen to 6,315 thirty years later. As early as 1914 the school built by Henry Fownes Luttrell II in 1866 was no longer large enough for the increasing number of children. A new one was built for boys, while the girls had to make do with the old one. In 1929 a grammar school was opened, and extended in 1938 to offer education to 400 pupils between the ages of ten and nineteen.

The Luttrell Memorial Hospital opened in 1867 was similarly too small for the district it served, and so in 1920 the Town Hall designed by Piers St Aubyn in the 1880s was converted into the Minehead and District Hospital.

In the early 'twenties a great deal was done to provide entertainment for visitors. On the sea front there was now the Queen's Hall, which could seat about 850 people for plays, concerts or film shows. The Cosy Cinema in Bancks Street held 350; it announced 'High Class Programmes of all the latest Pictures. Once Nightly. Matinees as advertised'. There was the Promenade Green near the station and the Summer Pavilion, offering music and variety shows; band concerts were given in the open air on the Green. Before long the Cosy Cinema was outgrown; the Regal Theatre and Cinema, which included a dance hall, opened in 1934. It was built on the site of a former tannery, the smell of which residents were not sorry to lose when it was pulled down in 1932. Blenheim Meadow had been prettified into Blenheim Gardens, where bands played, as they still do today.

Guide books referred visitors to the golf course on the Warren, to the east of the town. It had been established in 1882 as a nine-hole course by a local doctor named Clark, a Scotsman who was said to have been 'on the look-out for a suitable ground on which to play his national game' since his arrival in the area. At the end of the 19th century it was extended to 18 holes.

The harbour was by no means idle in the 'twenties and 'thirties; quite apart from small pleasure boats, there were still a few sailing coasters, including the *Emma Louise*, trading with South Wales, bringing in coal for the gasworks and for domestic use and taking back pit props.

Polo matches on Dunster Lawns were revived not long after the First World War, and continued until the eve of the Second; the usual annual tournament was held in August 1939. It was during these inter-war years that the Maharajah of Jodhpur was a frequent visitor; the town's annual guide remarked that his team was a 'huge attraction' and included spirited photographs of Indian syces cantering his ponies at exercise on Minehead beach. In 1925 the *West Somerset Free Press* reported that he had offered to present the West Somerset Polo Club with a new pavilion – provided that it did not cost more than £600. Matches were once more played on Wednesday and Saturday afternoons; by this time it was a motor bus from Hardy's Garage, not a

61. Polo on Dunster Lawns, below the castle. The magnificent stables of the castle last echoed with the clatter of hooves when the Maharajah of Jodhpur stabled his string of polo ponies in them in the years between the two World Wars.

horse-drawn brake, that carried spectators to the ground. In April 1925 the *Free Press* described the arrival of the Jodhpur Polo Team by special train, with 51 ponies said to be worth £15,000. The players stayed at the *Metropole*, while 'natives' were billeted at the *Pier Hotel*. For the autumn tournament, the fifth since the war, a Rajah Hanut Singh brought 15 ponies, attended by several syces. The season ended with a splendid ball at the *Metropole*.

The changes brought about by the outbreak of war in 1939 were far more abrupt and inescapable than those of 25 years earlier. Trains arriving at Minehead station were suddenly found to be crowded, not with holidaymakers, but with evacuees: hundreds of women with babies and children below school age arrived without warning, in addition to school-children for whom accommodation had been arranged well in advance. Billeting officers worked non-stop to try to find somewhere for the unexpected newcomers to stay.

As in so many other places, a drift back to the cities was seen during the months of the 'phoney war', but when air raids became severe in 1941, thousands more fled westwards on any available train, and a large number chose Minehead as their destination. It was estimated that at one time the population of the town had swollen to twenty thousand. Large houses were taken over, and the Urban District Council requisitioned all empty properties under a compulsory billeting order; even disused workhouses in the West Somerset area were re-opened as temporary accommodation.[3]

The Campbells' paddle steamers had once more gone to war – and sadly, the elegant promenade pier bought nearly twenty years earlier was demolished as part of coastal defence measures. As a result, when peace came, there was no possibility of a quick resumption of excursions by sea, as there had been in 1919.

Thus, although the Campbells took delivery of a new paddler, the *Bristol Queen*, in 1946, and Ilfracombe and other resorts were able to give her a jubilant welcome in September of that year, Minehead was forced to watch her sail to and fro without calling, as they had watched her predecessors in the 1890s.

However, at the beginning of 1951, Mr. Geoffrey Luttrell, with what seems a somewhat quixotic generosity, handed over the harbour and its old stone jetty to the Urban District Council. In his presentation speech he made a joking reference to the fact that he had charged the Council the sum of two pounds for the jetty, as no public body took proper care of anything given free. He allowed them to lease the harbour for 999 years at an annual rent of ten pounds.

As so often in the past, shingle banks had begun to block the harbour. These were cleared, and on the day of the official presentation the *Glen Usk* was able to berth alongside the jetty – the first White Funnel ship to call since August 1939. She was met off the coast by a flotilla of local craft decked with bunting, the *Emma Louise* among them.

Yet as the years passed, the Campbells' fleet dwindled away; one after another of the majestic paddlers was sold off or scrapped, and in the 1970s the only vessel the company was operating in the Bristol Channel was the M.V. *Balmoral*. In 1981 even she was withdrawn and taken north to be used as a floating restaurant in Dundee. In 1984 the Paddle Steamer Preservation Society managed to buy her, and appealed for funds to refit her for a return to her old station. Local authorities on both sides of the Bristol Channel contributed and, in May 1986, she was again sailing between ports along western coasts, visiting Penarth, Newport, Barry Island, Minehead, Ilfracombe and Lundy.

During the years of the *Balmoral*'s absence there had been just one vessel to offer day cruises to holidaymakers for a few weeks in summer. The paddle steamer *Waverley*, not the Campbells' original Clipper of the Clyde but one of her successors, had been operating in the Clyde. In 1973 she was bought by the Scottish branch of the Paddle Steamer Preservation Society, which soon decided to maintain traditional links with the south-west by means of summer visits. Even with the return of the *Balmoral*, these will continue.

One of the most unwelcome events in the continuing sequence of changes that had gone on almost decade by decade since Victorian times, was the closing of the branch line from Minehead to Taunton in January 1971. Immediately, the people of West Somerset showed that they had no intention of meekly acquiescing in the loss of this useful and attractive line. A month after the closure, a public meeting was held to consider what could be done. It was decided that, if possible, the railway should be re-opened and run by a private company.

Over the next five years the new West Somerset Railway Company managed to overcome all the difficulties of such an undertaking. The Somerset County Council helped greatly by buying the line and leasing it to the company, which then obtained the necessary Light Railway Transfer Order in July 1975. The track was brought back to a safe condition, defective parts being repaired or replaced. As soon as the line was re-opened as far as Blue Anchor in March 1976, the company went public, with an initial issue of tenpenny shares which subscribed over £95,000.

Later the service was extended to Bishops Lydeard. From there, any passengers wanting to travel to Taunton have to go by bus; for various reasons, partly financial, British Rail does not yet allow the operators of the line which they had consigned to oblivion to link with the main rail network by taking their trains the last five miles into Taunton station. However, most summer visitors probably go along for the ride, literally, in steam trains that amble along, swaying gently, to cover the 20 miles to Bishops Lydeard in about an hour.

As they slide out of Minehead station they pass, on the seaward side, a high wire boundary fence. Inside, partly screened by trees, is a complex of buildings and car

62. (*above*) Minehead jetty; the final sturdy structure – but in the 1930s the harbour lies empty save for the *Emma Louise*.

63. (*below*) After Minehead harbour had ceased to be busy with cargoes carried in sailing ships, paddle steamers began to bring a new type of trade, that of the summer tourist. Here one of the last paddlers in existence, the *Waverley*, goes astern as she leaves Minehead's often rebuilt stone jetty after a visit in the summer of 1985.

64. (*opposite above*) Dunster station in the 1980s.

65. (*opposite below*) A picture that might almost belong to the heyday of the original West Somerset Railway: a restored locomotive (Bagnall 0-6-0 Saddle Tank *Victor*, built for the British Steel Corporation about 1950) about to leave Minehead. Most of BBC 2's programmes 'Country Train' and 'Jazz Train' were filmed on this long platform. The West Somerset line, its rolling stock and stations have been seen by millions: they appeared in the Beatle's film 'A Hard Day's Night', in 'The Belstone Fox', and in television series including 'The Flockton Flyer', 'Shoestring' and 'A Question of Guilt'.

# THE ALL GAS KITCHEN

### THE LAST WORD IN DOMESTIC
### — HYGIENE AND ECONOMY. —

THE Gas Cooker is clean, reliable, and thoroughly efficient. Fuel consumption can be automatically limited to the minimum required to do the cooking "to a turn."

The Gas Water-Heater provides an ever-ready supply of hot water at any moment, day or night—and with the same economy of fuel. A Gas (or coke-fired) Incinerator and a Gas (or coke-fired) Washing Copper complete the installation. The former is a perfectly hygienic means of reducing refuse, wet or dry, to a clean and harmless ash ; the latter bids fair to revolutionise "washing day" in working and middle-class families—and, like the Incinerator, is one of those recent inventions that do most to promote sanitary conditions in the home.

*The Company are prepared to fix all kinds of Gas Apparatus and to supply Coke (delivered) and Tar.*

## Minehead Gas Light & Coke Co., Ltd.

Secretary & Manager : F. P. VINCE, The Gas Works.
Telephones : Works, 67 ; Showrooms, 109.

66. An advertisement from a Guide Book of the 1920s.

parks covering some dozen acres: Minehead's Butlins. At the end of 1960 Billy Butlin applied for permission to build a holiday camp to the east of the town, adjoining the golf course. Holding a special meeting on 30 December 1960, the Somerset County Council hastened to approve his plan.

The people of the town heard of the decision with mixed feelings and, not surprisingly, a public enquiry was called for. A headline in the *West Somerset Free Press* for 13 May 1961, reported 'Minehead Out in Force for Butlin Inquiry'. In spite of all objections, the go-ahead was given so quickly that by September the newspaper was printing pictures showing the first buildings going up on the site. Although Billy Butlin was quoted as saying at the inquiry that the camp would be comparatively small, it is now proclaimed as the largest in the country: 'Butlin's Flagship'. The word 'camp' has been dropped in favour of holiday centre; under the ownership of the Rank Organisation, it has been renamed Somerwest World.

Before reaching Dunster station, train passengers can see the Conygar Tower, almost submerged in foliage in summer, and the great seaward face of Dunster Castle. A long line of conifers hides the Hawn, once Dunster Haven. From Dunster to Blue Anchor the line runs near the sea before swinging inland to Washford. It returns to the coast at Watchet and then turns south-east to the agreeable little town of Williton, the home of the *West Somerset Free Press* and, since 1974, the headquarters of the West Somerset District Council. A few trains go only as far as this, but most make the full journey to Bishops Lydeard station which, like several on this line, stands at a distance from the village it serves. It is adorned with enamelled tin posters of the 'twenties and 'thirties, advertising such products as Petters Oil Engines, Pratts Motor Oil, Black Cat Cigarettes and Bryant and May matches. The Board of Trade Labour Exchange of Victoria Street, Bristol, announces that 'employers requiring workpeople and workpeople requiring employment should apply at the above address. No fee'.

The West Somerset Railway is said to be the longest privately-owned and operated passenger-carrying railway in Great Britain, and the only one offering a service to travellers all the year round.[4] In summer especially, running through the Quantocks borderland between very green fields where black and white Friesians and glossy horses graze, between sandstone banks and cuttings of rich raddle red and through tunnels of broad-leaved woodland, it creates the illusion of being a branch line of the past, on which passengers may slip back into the illusory tranquillity of late Victorian and Edwardian holidays.

It is an illusion soon dispelled on coming back into Minehead, even though many of its buildings belong to the period between 1880 and 1914. The harbour, except when the *Balmoral* or the *Waverley* call, is used only by small pleasure craft and a few fishing vessels, and Quay Town has become a row of neat, renovated cottages. At the far end of the Esplanade the *Metropole*, built as Minehead's Victorian luxury hotel, is partly flats, partly a pub, the *Hobby Horse Inn*. By contrast the *Beach Hotel* opposite the station, that once advertised good stabling for hunters, is still in business as a hotel. From the station, the Avenue and its continuation, the Parade, still run straight to Wellington Square, as they did a century ago, but now are fringed with a candy floss of cheap clothes shops, gift shops and places to eat.

Apart from the harbour, only the area round Middle Street, Church Street and Church Steps conveys some sense of the older past. Page, standing near St Michael's church in the late 1880s, deplored the way the town was spreading out, but he could still see it as possessing its historic three parts, Upper, Lower and Quay Towns. A visitor today would be unlikely to guess that they were once distinct. Not only have they become one continuous built-up area, but, in a mere half-century, building has engulfed the ancient hamlets of Periton and Woodcombe as, earlier, it had engulfed Alcombe. Looking south-east from the head of the path that winds down from North Hill through bracken, furze and heather to Woodcombe, one may see that only a few open fields lie between the houses most recently built beyond Alcombe Cross and the wooded cone of Conygar Hill that hides Dunster. John Fownes Luttrell's project of 1832, to build as far as Dunster to the east, as well as nearly two miles westwards, to save Minehead from being disfranchised, has now, for different reasons, almost come about. If the building rate of recent decades were maintained, Dunster would be enclosed within a lava flow of brick by the early 21st century.

To the west, the prospect is different. In 1944, the great Holnicote Estate, some 12,500 acres of farms, moorland and woods, was given to the National Trust by Sir Richard Acland, 'partly as a matter of principal, and partly to preserve them intact for future generations'. Less than thirty years earlier the 12th Baronet, Sir Thomas Dyke Acland, had similarly wished to safeguard Dunkery, and entered into an agreement with the Trust which enabled it to lease for 500 years not only Dunkery but parts of North Hill, of the Horner and Sweetworthy valleys, and moorland on Winsford Hill – some seven or eight thousand acres in all.[5] With the recent acquisition of Greenaleigh Farm, that centre for Victorian junketing parties, the Trust now protects a wide tract of north-east Exmoor stretching back from North Hill to Dunkery.

Although it has its beaches and harbour, and Somerwest World for those who seek ready-made entertainment, it is clear that Minehead, choosing to make much of its living from tourism, sees the moor as a large part of its attraction. The roadside signboard that today welcomes anyone approaching the town from the east carries the words 'Gateway to Exmoor National Park'. At least two other of the moor's perimeter towns, South Molton and Dulverton, look on themselves as similar gateways, but those of course lie inland. For the first century or so of its development as a seaside resort, Minehead regarded the moor primarily as a draw for those who wanted to hunt; until at least the Second World War, guide books made much of its convenience for meets of staghounds, foxhounds and harriers. Of the killing sports, only fishing has a place in the contemporary guide to Minehead and West Somerset.[6] Horse riding is listed among 'things to do', but hunting is not.

The Exmoor National Park Authority's free newspaper, *The Exmoor Visitor*, recommends the moor to visitors as 'a place where time runs slowly'. Today it is perhaps because, in both Dunster and Minehead, there is a sense that time runs slowly that they are places where life runs well.

67. The wild red deer of Exmoor (Jeboult).

# Minehead's M.P.s, 1562-1832

**Elizabeth I**

| | |
|---|---|
| 1562-3 | Thomas Luttrell |
| | Thomas Fitzwilliams |
| 1572 | Dominick Chester |
| 1584 | No return given for Minehead Borough |
| 1586 | John Luttrell |
| | Robert Crosse |
| 1588-9 | Benedict Baynham |
| | John Luttrell |
| 1592-3 | James Quirke, merchant |
| | Richard Hanbury |
| 1597 | Amias Bampfilde |
| | Conrad Prowse |
| 1601 | Francis James |
| | Lewis Lashbrooke |

**James I**

| | |
|---|---|
| 1603-4 | Sir Ambrose Turville |
| | Sir Maurice Barkley |
| 1614 | No return found |
| 1620-1 | No return found |
| 1623-4 | Sir Arthur Lake |
| | Arthur Ducke |

**Charles I**

| | |
|---|---|
| 1625 | Thomas Luttrell |
| | Edmund Wyndham |
| 1625-6 | Sir John Gill |
| | Thomas Horner |
| 1627-8 | Edmund Wyndham |
| | Thomas Horner |
| 1640 | Francis Wyndham |
| | Alexander Popham, who was also elected for Bath, and chose that seat in preference to Minehead |
| | Arthur Ducke, replacing Alexander Popham |

**Long Parliament**

Sir Francis Popham
Alexander Luttrell
Edward Popham
Walter Strickland

**Interregnum**

No Minehead representatives were returned for the parliaments of 1653, 1654 and 1656, but Francis Luttrell was one of the 11 members for Somerset in the parliament of 1656-8, as was Alexander Popham (above)

**Richard Cromwell**

| | |
|---|---|
| 1658-9 | Richard Hutchinson, who after election did not in fact represent Minehead, choosing Rochester instead |

**Charles II**

| | |
|---|---|
| 1660 | Francis Luttrell |
| | Charles Pym |
| 1661 | Francis Luttrell |
| | Sir Hugh Wyndham |
| | On the death of Francis Luttrell, John Malet was elected; on the death of Sir Hugh Wyndham, Thomas Wyndham was elected |
| 1678-9 | Francis Luttrell (born 1659, son of Francis Luttrell above) |
| | Sir John Malet |
| 1679 | Francis Luttrell |
| | Thomas Palmer |
| 1680-1 | Francis Luttrell |
| | Thomas Palmer |

**James II**

| | |
|---|---|
| 1685 | Francis Luttrell |
| | Nathaniel Palmer |
| 1688-9 | Francis Luttrell |
| | Nathaniel Palmer |

**William and Mary**

| | |
|---|---|
| 1689-90 | Col. Francis Luttrell |
| | Nathaniel Palmer, who elected to serve for the county of Somerset, as he continued to do during the reigns of William III and Anne. John Sandford was elected in his place in |

1690. On the death of Col. Francis
Luttrell in the same year, his brother
Col. Alexander Luttrell was elected

## William III
1695      Alexander Luttrell
          John Sandford
1698      Alexander Luttrell
          Jacob Bancks

## Anne
1700-1    Alexander Luttrell
          Sir Jacob Bancks (married Mary, the
          widow of Col. Francis Luttrell II, in
          1696; knighted in 1699)
1702      Alexander Luttrell
          Sir Jacob Bancks
1705      Alexander Luttrell
          Sir Jacob Bancks
1708      Sir Jacob Bancks
          Sir John Trevelyan, who also repre-
          sented the county of Somerset in the
          parliaments of 1695-8 and 1701
1710 &    Sir Jacob Bancks
1713      Sir John Trevelyan

## George I
1714-15   Sir John Trevelyan
          Sir William Wyndham, who was to
          serve as M.P. for Somerset from
          1715 until his death in 1740, despite
          a spell of some months in the Tower
          for planning a rising in the West in
          favour of the Stuarts. As the election
          of Sir John Trevelyan was declared
          void, James Milner was elected in
          his place. On Milner's death, Robert
          Mansell was elected
1722      Thomas Hales
          Robert Mansell. On Mansell's
          death, Francis Whitworth was elec-
          ted in his place
1727      Francis Whitworth
          Alexander Luttrell. On his death in
          1737, Sir William Codrington re-
          placed him, and on Codrington's
          death Thomas Carew of Crowcombe
          was elected

## George II
1741      Thomas Carew
          Francis Whitworth. On Whitworth's
          death John Periam replaced him
1747      Percy Wyndham O'Brien
          Charles Whitworth

1754      Charles Whitworth
          Daniel Boone

## George III
1761      Percy, Earl of Thomond
          Henry Shiffner
1768      Henry Fownes Luttrell
          Charles Whitworth
1774      Henry Fownes Luttrell
          John Fownes Luttrell. Henry
          Fownes Luttrell applied for the Chil-
          tern Hundreds in 1774, and Thomas
          Pownall of North and West Lynn
          was elected in his place
1780      John Fownes Luttrell
          Francis Fownes Luttrell, who ap-
          plied for the Chiltern Hundreds in
          1783; Henry Beaufoy of Shropshire
          was elected in his place
1784      John Fownes Luttrell
          Henry Beaufoy, who elected to serve
          for Great Yarmouth. Charles Phipps
          was elected in his place; on Phipps'
          death, Robert Wood replaced him
1793      John Fownes Luttrell
          Viscount Parker. On the Viscount's
          call to the Upper House as Earl of
          Macclesfield, Thomas Fownes Lut-
          trell was elected in his place
1796 (first parliament of the United Kingdom)
          John Fownes Luttrell
          John Langston
1802      John Fownes Luttrell
          John Patteson
1806      Sir John Lethbridge, who applied for
          the Chiltern Hundreds in 1807, and
          was replaced by John Fownes Lut-
          trell
          Baron Rancliffe of Ireland
1807      John Fownes Luttrell
          John Denison of Ossington, Notts
1812      John Fownes Luttrell
          John Fownes Luttrell the younger
          In 1816 Henry Fownes Luttrell was
          elected in place of John Fownes
          Luttrell the elder
1818      John Fownes Luttrell
          Henry Fownes Luttrell
1820      John Fownes Luttrell
          Henry Fownes Luttrell, who applied
          for the Chiltern Hundreds in 1822.
          John Douglas of Grantham, in Lin-
          colnshire, was elected in his place

**George IV**

1826        John Fownes Luttrell
            James Blair of Wigtown

**William IV**

1830        John Fownes Luttrell
            William Edward Tomline of Riby
            Grove, Lincolnshire
1831        John Fownes Luttrell
            Viscount Villiers of Middleton Park,
            Oxford

1832        Minehead defranchised by the Re-
            form Bill
1833        Redistribution of seats:
            Somerset, Eastern Division
            Somerset, Western Division
            Bath City
            Bridgwater Borough
            Frome Borough
            Taunton Borough
            Wells City

# The Incumbents of St Michael's Church, Minehead, c.1200-1987

| Date of Institution | Incumbent | Patron |
|---|---|---|
| c.1200 | Godfrey | |
| c.1287 | Robert Dolthrop | |
| 1313 | Gilbert Pyro | Prior of Bruton |
| 1348 | John Toker | Prior of Bruton |
| | Mattheus Eliot | Prior of Bruton |
| 1401 | Richard Bruton | Prior of Bruton |
| 1406 | Thomas Benet | Prior of Bruton |
| 1408 | John Hansford | Prior of Bruton |
| 1419 | Reginald Smyth | Prior of Bruton |
| 1434 | Thomas Warr | Prior of Bruton |
| 1437 | Robert Cammell | Prior of Bruton |
| | William Barbour | Prior of Bruton |
| 1484 | Richard Fitzjames | Prior of Bruton |
| 1497 | Henry Sutton, M.D. | Archbishop of Canterbury |
| 1500 | John Pykeman | |
| 1502 | Thomas Beaumont | |
| 1507 | William Gilbert | Richard, Abbot of Glastonbury, and the Prior of Bridgwater |
| 1526 | Walter Cretyng, LL.D | |
| 1533 | John Richards | |
| 1561 | John Tilly | John Fry |
| 1562 | Thomas Williams | Queen Elizabeth I |
| 1585 | Nicholas Prowse | |
| 1635 | Robert Knolles | Maria Prowse, widow of Nicholas Prowse |
| 1637 | George Glasden (Dunster Castle Papers) | |
| 1660 | Nicholas Prowse | Nicholas Prowse |
| 1666 | Samuel Rooke | Anna Prowse, widow of Nicholas Prowse |
| 1686 | Theophilus Downes | Samuel Crockford |
| 1687 | Samuel Bengoe | Thomas Cornish |
| 1693 | Robert Stone | Samuel Crockford |
| 1702 | Tristram Chave | Joanna Stone, widow of Robert Stone |
| 1709 | William Moggridge | Joanna Chave, widow of Tristram Chave |
| 1763 | Leonard Herring | Henry Fownes Luttrell |
| 1776 | Peter Woodley | Henry Fownes Luttrell |
| 1780 | Alexander F. Luttrell | John Fownes Luttrell |
| 1816 | George Henry Leigh | John Fownes Luttrell |
| 1829 | Thomas Luttrell | John Fownes Luttrell |
| 1832 | Alexander F. Luttrell | John Fownes Luttrell |

| 1899 | Francis M. Etherington | George Fownes Luttrell |
| 1914 | Edward Parry Liddon | Alexander Fownes Luttrell |
| 1935 | George E. Knapp-Fisher | Alexander Fownes Luttrell |
| 1946 | Ronald D. G. Bennett | George Fownes Luttrell |
| 1952 | Ernest C. Mortimer | George Fownes Luttrell |
| 1960 | Frank L. M. Bennett, M.A. | Archbishop of Canterby by lapse. sede vacante |
| 1967 | C. Leslie Ward, Prebendary of Wells Cathedral | Lt. Col. Walter Luttrell, M.C. |
| 1976 | Christopher H. Saralis | Lt. Col. Walter Luttrell, M.C. |

# The Minehead Hobby Horse

Like Padstow, Minehead has long possessed a Hobby Horse which parades the
town at the beginning of May. The earliest
published reference to Minehead's Horse
appeared in 1830 in Savage's *A History of
Carhampton*; he says that the young men,
mostly fishermen and sailors, made 'some
grotesque figures of light stuff, rudely
resembling men, and horses with long
tails'. With these, they perambulated the
town and neighbourhood, 'performing a
variety of antics ... they never fail to pay a
visit to Dunster Castle, where, after
having been hospitably regaled with
strong beer and victuals, they always
receive a present of money'. Since then
there have been occasional prophecies
that the custom was dying out, but even
during the First World War, while their
elders were serving elsewhere, it was
carried on by youths.

68. Although no published record of Minehead's
Hobby Horse is known before 1830, its origins
would almost certainly have gone back into the
18th century, and possibly much earlier. In this
photograph, taken on 1 May 1984, the Horse
pauses on the corner by the SWEB showrooms
which are a regrettable substitute for the old inn,
the *Plume of Feathers*.

Yet in general, the people of Minehead
do not seem to have much interest in or
affection for their Horse or Horses (there
are usually two). A visitor to Minehead on
1 May may walk a long way before finding
the Sailors' Horse and its few attendants. The contrast with Padstow, where
whole-hearted, day-long celebrations fill the town with singing and rejoicing and
draw crowds of visitors to share in the fun, is striking. Perhaps the music has
something to do with it. Padstow's Morning Song and Day Song, with their strong
rhythms and subtly varying tunes, are familiar to most Cornish and adopted Cornish
people; probably their many verses are known by heart by a fair number, and the
chorus of the Morning Song ('sung anywhere ad lib' as one copy puts it) certainly is.
    H. W. Kille, who wrote a paper in 1931 for the Somerset Archaeological and
Natural History Society on 'West Country Hobby Horses and Cognate Customs',

said that in the 19th century Minehead's Horse was accompanied by as many as four clarionet players and sometimes brass instruments, as well as a drummer. Today it cavorts to an elusive thread of melody, played on an accordion and drum; there seem to be no words. For the most part, passers-by take no notice of it; only when the Sailors' Horse and the Alcombe Horse meet in the evening in Wellington Square does a crowd collect to watch them.

69. Original version of the 'Sailor's Hobby Horse'.

# Notes

## Chapter One

1. W. Boyd Dawkins, 'Early Man', *Victoria County History of Somerset*, Vol. 1, London, 1906.
2. There is another Bury Castle, near Dulverton, described by Charles Whybrow in *Antiquary's Exmoor* as 'an evident Norman motte-and-bailey about which nothing at all is known'.
3. Gilbert H. Doble, *The Saints of Cornwall*, Part 4, Truro, 1965. The 10th Report of the Historical Manuscripts Commission (Appendix part 6, p. 73) mentions a church of St Karentoc near the King's Highway in Carhampton.
4. It was one of only two Norman castles in Somerset; the other was Montacute.
5. Eilert Ekwall, *The Concise Dictionary of English Place-Names*, 4th edition, O.U.P., 1960. Thomas Gerard, in 1633, was more discerning than later topographical writers when he wrote that the name must 'surely come from ye Brittaynes Myndde, which imports as much as an hill or mountain'.
6. According to Sir H. C. Maxwell Lyte, this was William de Mohun II. Collinson, however, interposes a generation between William de Mohun I and the rebel against Stephen, referring to him as a person of great valour who improved the buildings of his predecessors at Dunster. Certainly if Maxwell Lyte is correct in saying that William II was still alive in 1142, he must have been a man well into his sixties when Stephen came to the throne, unless he was born very late in the lifetime of a father who was a follower of the Conqueror.
7. Edward T. MacDermot, *A History of the Forest of Exmoor*, edited by Roger Sellick (David and Charles, 1973).

## Chapter Two

1. Inquisition post mortem on John de Mohun, 1279.
2. If Hancock is correct in assuming that the vague dating '28 Edward' refers to Edward I and not Edward III.
3. Although the *Victoria County History of Somerset* observes that in Somerset, those who held in villeinage are usually classified as virgaters who cultivated 30 acres, half-virgaters with 15 acres, ferdellers who held a ferdel or furlong and cotters with about five acres, it is clear that on the Minehead Manor, a virgate (a quarter of a hide) amounted to 48 acres, and the smaller holdings were fractions of that figure.
4. It is interesting that in 1971 a new vineyard of 500 vines was planted at Rhyll Manor, near Dulverton, to grow grapes for white wine. See essay by Gilliam Pearkes, *Exmoor Review*, 1973.
5. It is now in the British Museum.
6. Inquisition post mortem on John de Mohun, 1330.
7. Preb. E. H. Bates Harbin, *The Black Death in Somersetshire, 1348-9*, Somerset Archaeological and Natural History Society, Vol. 63, 1917. The Rev. J. F. Chanter ('The Court Rolls of the Manor of Curry Rivel, 1348-9', *S.A. & N.H.S.* Vol. 56, 1917) observes that Ralph de Salopia, Bishop of Bath and Wells, ordered special prayers and ceremonies in August 1348, to seek divine protection from 'the pestilence which has come from the east'. As these were unavailing, in January 1349, he recorded in a pastoral letter that many Somerset parishes were left destitute of clergy, and therefore advised any sick person in such a parish to confess his or her sins to a layman; if a man was not at hand 'even to a woman'.
8. See *Minehead, a History of the Parish, Manor and Port*, by Preb. F. Hancock, for his transcription of this document and others quoted in this and the succeeding chapter.

9. There are several references to the Byrcombe Chapel in the Luttrell accounts. Sir Hugh visited it in October 1405, which must have been very soon after he returned from France to claim his inheritance; his steward noted an outlay of twelve pence 'for the expenses of the lord going abroad to the Chapel of the Holy Trinity at Bircombe'. At Michaelmas 1419, a monk called Johanni Buryton, who was apparently chaplain at Dunster Castle, received what was probably his regular stipend of just over £3, together with nearly £2 for celebrating mass at 'Bycomb' for a year at the wish of the lord. Twelve months later his ordinary stipend has not changed, but now the payment for celebrating mass at Byrcombe Chapel has risen almost four-fold. Had Johanni been complaining of the hardships of travelling out again and again to the tiny isolated chapel on the cliffs? A rent roll of 1505 shows that a Richard Boys paid fourpence for '1 Boathouse under chapel'; perhaps this was on the shore below the Burgundy Chapel. Reports of excavations carried out at the chapel in 1984 and 1985 appear in the West Somerset Archaeological and Natural History Society's Newsletters Nos. 7 and 10.

### Chapter Four

1. The full text of the contract agreed between John Marys and the Dunster parishioners appears as an appendix to Sir H. C. Maxwell Lyte's *Dunster and Its Lords*.
2. Alfred C. Fryer, *Monumental Effigies in Somerset*, Som. Arch. and N.H. Soc., Vol. 63, 1917.
3. Memorial brasses to the historians of Dunster and Minehead, Sir Henry Maxwell Lyte and Preb. Frederick Hancock, are to be seen in Dunster church. Preb. Hancock graduated at Wadham in 1872. He was Rector of Selworthy from 1884 until 1898 and subsequently Vicar of Dunster, Rural Dean of Dunster and Prebendary of Wells Cathedral. His *History of Minehead* was published in 1903 and his *History of Dunster Church and Priory* in 1905. He also wrote a history of Selworthy. Sir Henry Maxwell Lyte was a descendant of the Lytes of Lytes Cary. He was Deputy Keeper of the Records from 1886 until 1926. He died in 1940 in his 93rd year. I have been indebted to the works of both these authors in writing several chapters of this book.
4. Or William de Mohun V: see note 6, Chapter One.
5. According to Hancock, 'After the dissolution of Bruton Priory, the advowson of Minehead seems to have led a shuttlecock kind of existence'. It was successively in the hands of Henry VIII, Edward VI, Elizabeth I and James I, and later had lay or clerical owners. In 1717 it passed to the Luttrells, when Mrs. Dorothy Luttrell paid £250 and two broad pieces of gold for it on behalf of her son Alexander.
6. F. W. Weaver, editor, *Somerset Medieval Wills* (Alan Sutton, 1983).

### Chapter Five

1. Somerset and Dorset *Notes and Queries*, Vol. I, p. 261.
2. Bristol Channel Shipping; cross-channel voyages between Welsh ports and those in ... West Somerset recorded in the Welsh Port Books, 1560-1603. North Devon Athenaeum Mss.
3. Preb. Hancock, *op. cit.*
4. F. W. Weaver, *op. cit.*
5. Bristol Channel Shipping, 1560-1603.
6. Letters and Papers of Henry VIII, Vol. I.
7. The Rev. John Collinson remarked that he 'wasted the fair patrimony that descended to him from his ancestors', but Maxwell Lyte considered this rather strong.

### Chapter Six

1. M. M. Oppenheim, 'Maritime History', *Victoria County History of Somerset*, Vol. 2, Constable, 1911.
2. Cal. State Papers Domestic, Charles I, 1630-4.
3. Cal. State Papers Domestic, Charles I, 1634.
4. David Underhill, *Somerset in the Civil War and Interregnum*, (David and Charles, 1973).

5. The document is reproduced in full in Hancock's *Minehead*.

6. Somerset and Dorset *Notes and Queries*, Vol. 19.


*Chapter Seven*

1. F. J. Snell, *The Book of Exmoor* (Methuen, 1903).

2. Rev. John Collinson, *The History of Somerset* (Bath, 1791).

3. Rev. James Savage, *A History of the Hundred of Carhampton* (Bristol and London, 1830).

4. Ethel M. Hewitt, 'The Textile Industry', *Victoria County History of Somerset*, Vol. II.

5. Somerset and Dorset *Notes and Queries*, Vol. 30, 1976, pp. 187 and 191.

6. Cal. State Papers Domestic, Charles I, 1646.

7. Hancock, *op. cit.*

8. Cal. State Papers Domestic, Interregnum, 1655.

9. M. M. Oppenheim, *op. cit.*

10. Cal. State Papers Domestic, Charles II, 1667.

11. Historical Manuscripts Commission, Part 6, 1887.

12. *Dictionary of National Biography*.

13. *The Western Martyrology* lists three men of Dunster (Henry Lackwell, John Geanes and William Sully) and six men of Minehead (John Jones, alias Evans, Hugh Starke, Francis Bartlett, Peter Warren, Samuel Hawkins and Richard Sweet) as being condemned to death by Judge Jefferies after Monmouth's Rebellion.

14. Hancock, *op. cit.*

15. Somerset and Dorset *Notes and Queries*, Vol. 20.

16. Hancock, *op. cit.*

17. Historical Manuscripts Commission, Part 6, 1887.


*Chapter Eight*

1. Material for this chapter is largely derived from the extensive extracts from the churchwardens' accounts of Minehead and Dunster in Preb. Hancock's *Minehead* and his *History of Dunster Church and Priory*.

2. Grahame Farr, *Wreck and Rescue in the Bristol Channel* (D. Bradford Barton, 1966).


*Chapter Nine*

1. This survey is reproduced in Hancock's *Minehead*.

2. Rev. John Collinson, *op. cit.*

3. Benjamin Martin, *The Natural History of England*, London, 1759.

4. John Billingsley, *General View of the Agriculture of Somerset*, London, 1795.

5. Grahame Farr, 'Custom House Ship Registers in the West Country', *The South West and the Sea*, Exeter University, 1968.

6. *Universal British Directory of Trade and Commerce*, 5 vols., 1790-5.

7. As elsewhere, this warren dates back to Norman times. In the late 19th century it became the site of Minehead Golf Course. The name survives in Warren Point and Warren Road.

8. The Rev. Richard Warner, *A Walk Through some of the Western Counties of England*, 1800.

9. Richard Ayton and William Daniell, *A Voyage Round Great Britain*, Tate Gallery, 1978.

10. Charles G. Harper, *The Somerset Coast* (Chapman and Hall, 1909).


*Chapter Ten*

1. Preb. Hancock provides a full account of the electoral history of the town in Chapter Five, 'Political History' of his *Minehead*.

*Chapter Eleven*

1. Pigot and Co., *National Commercial Directory*, London, 1830.
2. *West Somerset Free Press*, July 1874.
3. *Minehead Advertiser and Visitors' List*, August 1887.
4. Charles Harper, *The Somerset Coast*, Chapman and Hall, 1909.
5. Grahame Farr, *Somerset Harbours*, Christopher Johnson, 1954.


*Chapter Twelve*

1. The garages included Hardy and Co. and Staddon and Co.
2. Arthur Heinemann, *Victoria County History of Somerset*, Vol. 2, 1911.
3. Jack Hurley, *Exmoor in Wartime*, Exmoor Press, 1978.
4. Allan Stanistreet, *West Somerset Railway Official Guide*, West Somerset Books, 1981.
5. Anne Acland, *A Devon Family: The Story of the Aclands*, Phillimore and Co. Ltd., 1981.
6. *Minehead and West Somerset Official Guide*, issued by the Minehead and West Somerset Publicity Association, Market House, The Parade, Minehead.

# Bibliography

Binding, Hilary and Stevens, Douglas, *A History of Minehead* (Exmoor Press, 1977)
Collinson, Rev. John, *The History of Somerset* (Bath, 1791)
*Domesday Book: Somerset*, edited by Caroline and Frank Thorn (Phillimore, 1980)
Dunning, Robert, *A History of Somerset* (Chichester, 1983).
Eeles, Francis C., *The Parish Church of St Michael, Minehead* (Taunton, 1926)
Farr, Grahame, *Somerset Harbours* (Christopher Johnson, 1954)
Gerard, Thomas, *A Particular Description of the County of Somerset* (Privately printed, 1633)
Grinsell, L. V., *The Archaeology of Exmoor* (David and Charles, 1970)
Hancock, Preb. Frederick, *Dunster Church and Priory* (Taunton, 1905)
– *Minehead, a History of the Parish, Manor and Port* (Privately printed, 1903)
Harper, Charles, *The Somerset Coast* (Chapman and Hall, 1909)
Hurley, Jack, *Exmoor in Wartime* (Exmoor Press, 1978)
Lyte, Sir H. C. Maxwell, *Dunster and Its Lords, 1066-1881* (Privately printed, 1882)
– *A History of Dunster*, 2 vols. (St Catherine Press, 1909)
Page, John Lloyd Warden, *An Exploration of Exmoor* (Seeley and Co. 1890)
Savage, Rev. James, *A History of the Hundred of Carhampton* (Bristol and London, 1830)
Stanistreet, Allan, *West Somerset Railway Official Guide* (West Somerset Books, 1981)
Underhill, David, *Somerset in the Civil War and Interregnum* (1973)
*Victoria County History of Somerset*, 2 vols. (Constable 1911)
Warner, Rev. Richard, *A Walk Through Some of the Western Counties of England* (1800)
Weaver, F. W., editor, *Somerset Medieval Wills* (Alan Sutton, 1983)

## Directories

*The Universal British Directory* (5 vols. 1793-1798)
*National Commercial Directory* (Pigot and Co., London, 1830)
*Royal National and Commercial Directory* (Pigot and Co., London, 1844)
*General Directory for the County of Somerset* (Taunton, 1840)
*Bristol Post Office Directory and Gazetteer* (1859)
*Post Office Directory of Somerset and Bristol* (1861)
*Commercial Directory* (Morris and Co., 1874)

## Guide Books

Larter, C. E., *Minehead, Porlock and Dunster* (Homeland Association Ltd., 20th edition, 1924)
*The Official Guide to Minehead* (Minehead Improvement and Publicity Association, c. 1920)
*Dunster Castle* (The National Trust, 1983)

## Printed Records

*The Muster Rolls of Somerset, 1569*, edited by Emmanuel Green (Somerset Record Society, 1904)

# Index

115

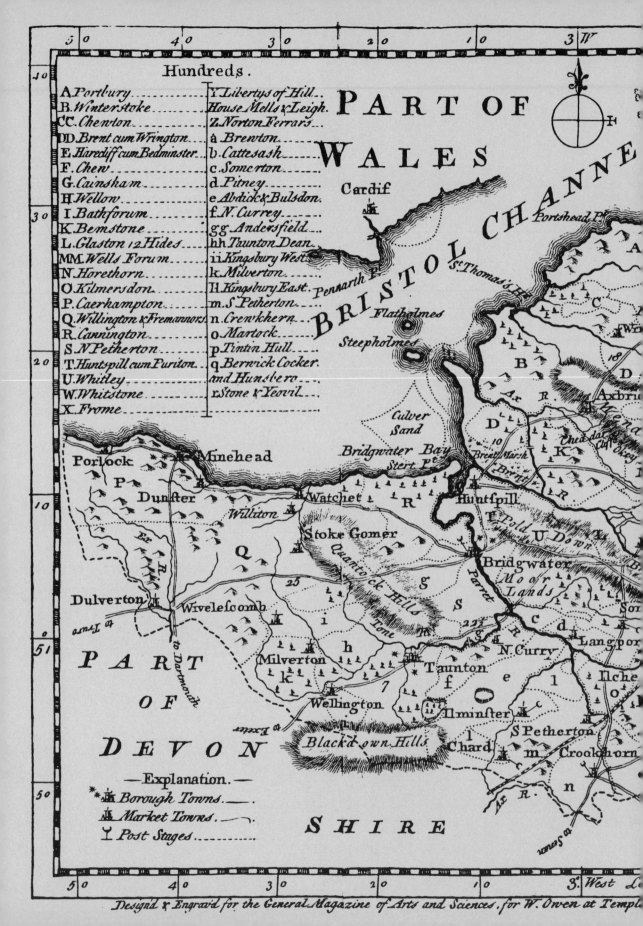